To:

From:

Date:

# A *Confidence* THAT CHANGES EVERYTHING

Devotions to Shine Bright
in This Topsy-Turvy Life

*Hannah Crews*

*A Confidence That Changes Everything: Devotions to Shine Bright in This Topsy-Turvy Life*
Copyright © 2025 Hannah Crews. All rights reserved.
First Edition, April 2025

Published by:

21154 Highway 16 East
Siloam Springs, AR 72761
dayspring.com

All rights reserved. *A Confidence That Changes Everything: Devotions to Shine Bright in This Topsy-Turvy Life* is under copyright protection. No part of this book may be used or reproduced in any manner whatsoever without written permission except in the case of brief quotations embodied in critical articles and reviews.

Scripture quotations marked NLT are taken from the Holy Bible, New Living Translation, copyright © 1996, 2004, 2015 by Tyndale House Foundation. Used by permission of Tyndale House Publishers, Inc., Carol Stream, Illinois 60188. All rights reserved.

Scripture quotations marked ESV are taken from The Holy Bible, English Standard Version. ESV® Text Edition: 2016. Copyright © 2001 by Crossway Bibles, a publishing ministry of Good News Publishers.

Scripture quotations marked NIV are taken from the Holy Bible, New International Version®, NIV®. Copyright © 1973, 1978, 1984, 2011 by Biblica, Inc.® Used by permission. All rights reserved worldwide.

Scripture quotations marked KJV are taken from the Holy Bible, King James Version.

Scripture quotations marked NKJV are taken from the New King James Version®. Copyright © 1982 by Thomas Nelson. Used by permission. All rights reserved.

Scripture quotations marked NASB1995 are taken from the NEW AMERICAN STANDARD BIBLE®, © Copyright 1960, 1962, 1963, 1968, 1971, 1972, 1973, 1975, 1977, 1995 by the Lockman Foundation. Used by permission. (www.lockman.org)

Scripture quotations marked CEV are from Contemporary English Version.® Copyright © 1995 American Bible Society. All rights reserved.

Written by: Hannah Crews
Cover Design by: Greg Jackson

Printed in China
Prime: U3368
ISBN: 979-8-88603-027-3

# Contents

Foreword . . . . . . . . . . . . . . . . . . . . . . . . . . . . . . . 9
Introduction . . . . . . . . . . . . . . . . . . . . . . . . . . . . . 11
Purpose Like a Pineapple . . . . . . . . . . . . . . . . . . . . 12
Confidence vs. Self-Esteem . . . . . . . . . . . . . . . . . . 14
Proceed with Confidence . . . . . . . . . . . . . . . . . . . 16
Conviction: A Grace Warning . . . . . . . . . . . . . . . . 18
"You Are Impressive" . . . . . . . . . . . . . . . . . . . . . . 20
Anything You Can Do, I Can Do Better . . . . . . . . . 22
Who Is God's Favorite? . . . . . . . . . . . . . . . . . . . . . 24
Ask the Hard Questions . . . . . . . . . . . . . . . . . . . . 26
Leave the Past at the Well . . . . . . . . . . . . . . . . . . 28
Triggered or Glimmered? . . . . . . . . . . . . . . . . . . . 30
Take Your Supplements! . . . . . . . . . . . . . . . . . . . 34
The Pessimist, The Optimist, & The Psalmist . . . . . 36
You're a Failure. Not! . . . . . . . . . . . . . . . . . . . . . . 38
Level Up! . . . . . . . . . . . . . . . . . . . . . . . . . . . . . . 40
God? Is That You? . . . . . . . . . . . . . . . . . . . . . . . . 42
Comparison Kills Confidence . . . . . . . . . . . . . . . . 44
You Gifted Girl, You! . . . . . . . . . . . . . . . . . . . . . . 46
Created in His Image . . . . . . . . . . . . . . . . . . . . . 48
The Gift of Exercise . . . . . . . . . . . . . . . . . . . . . . 50
A Confidence of Many Colors . . . . . . . . . . . . . . . 52
Praise Changes Things . . . . . . . . . . . . . . . . . . . . 56
When Our Bodies Fail . . . . . . . . . . . . . . . . . . . . . 58
Miss Dependent . . . . . . . . . . . . . . . . . . . . . . . . . 60

| | |
|---|---|
| The Domino Effect | 62 |
| Become a Student | 64 |
| Look at This Photograph | 66 |
| Be a Girl's Girl | 68 |
| Praying with Confidence | 70 |
| Discernment Boosts Confidence | 72 |
| The Most Important Devotion You'll Ever Read | 74 |
| Open and Closed Doors | 78 |
| Do It with All Your Heart | 80 |
| Conviction vs. Condemnation | 82 |
| Expecting the Worst | 84 |
| A Hugged Pot | 86 |
| A Black Cloud | 88 |
| The Snowball Effect of Joy | 90 |
| Observe, Regulate, Adjust | 92 |
| Answered and Unanswered | 94 |
| The Daily Seven | 96 |
| Operate in Your Gifts | 100 |
| Beware of Sharks | 102 |
| Oh Be Careful, Little Eyes | 104 |
| Have Fun! | 106 |
| Stimulate Wholesome Thinking | 108 |
| Unusual Wisdom | 110 |
| Be a Prepper | 112 |
| Blur the Distractions | 114 |
| I'm Not Cut Out for This! | 116 |
| The Heat of Pressure | 118 |

| | |
|---|---|
| Rest Is Best | 122 |
| Live to Give | 124 |
| It's How We Say It | 126 |
| The Bible Is a Mirror | 128 |
| Botrayal of Confidence | 130 |
| Choices, Choices | 132 |
| What Money Can't Buy | 134 |
| Chasing Approval | 136 |
| Discipline Brings Confidence | 138 |
| The Most Important Devotion You'll Ever Read...Again | 140 |
| Our Scars Are Our Witness | 144 |
| Identity in Christ | 146 |
| Calm, Cool, & Self-Controlled | 148 |
| Stop! Collaborate and Listen! | 150 |
| Be Bold | 152 |
| The Brightest in the Room | 154 |
| The New Kid on the Block | 156 |
| The Ultimate Trust Fall | 158 |
| The Ingredients List | 160 |
| Presence over Platform | 162 |
| The Struggle Is Real | 166 |
| Your Circle Matters | 168 |
| Zip It! | 170 |
| That's Totally About Me! | 172 |
| Am I an Imposter? | 174 |
| Don't Walk on Water...Yet | 176 |

| | |
|---|---|
| He Goes Before You | 178 |
| The Road to Repentance | 180 |
| Spiritual Vitality | 182 |
| The Confidence Language | 184 |
| Faith Is Confidence | 188 |
| A Reputation Above Reproach | 190 |
| Nobody Understands! | 192 |
| Candle Burning at Both Ends | 194 |
| Just My Luck! | 196 |
| Victory over Victimhood | 198 |
| Restore the Sparkle | 200 |
| Guilt-Free Confidence | 202 |
| The Only Way | 204 |
| A Confidence That Changes Everything | 206 |

# Foreword

If you've walked the earth long enough to read a magazine cover or scroll an Instagram feed, you've undoubtedly received messages telling you to be confident in yourself just because you're you. This idea of self-confidence feels absolutely beautiful and empowering—until you take note of all the other contradictory messages coming your way that subtly imply you need some improvements in order to feel confident in your own skin.

*"Be confident in your natural beauty, but make sure to have a flawless complexion."*

*"Be confident without trying, but make sure your house is designed for a magazine shoot."*

*"Be confident in your worth, but make sure to have investment properties by age thirty-five."*

We suddenly start seeking to achieve a worldly definition of confidence, yet we find ourselves losing confidence in the process of trying to attain it. All of it feels overwhelming, to put it lightly.

I recently learned a lesson on the dangers of seeking confidence by the world's standards when I woke up one morning with a paralyzed face from shingles and was told by doctors that I may never look like me again. The next day, I stared at my drooping face in the mirror with an eye that wouldn't shut and a mouth that didn't work on one side, realizing I had a decision to make:

Would I hide out, knowing my face wouldn't meet the world's beauty standards?

Or would I live with "God-fidence," knowing that my worth isn't determined by what the world says about me but instead by what God says about me?

As I read First Samuel 16:7 (NLT), "People judge by outward appearance, but the LORD looks at the heart," I consciously chose to take my focus off outward beauty and put my effort into making my heart beautiful by immersing myself in God's truths. The more I believed that I am beautiful because I am *His*, a confidence grew within me. I didn't have a smile on my face, but I could walk into a room with joy because my confidence didn't come from chasing after the world's approval. Instead, it came from chasing after *Him*.

Today, with my smile fully restored, I am excited to see how God restores your smile too. May my friend Hannah's words help you, encourage you, and lead you to discover a confidence that changes everything!

## Quinn Kelly

MRSQUINNKELLY.COM
INSTAGRAM.COM/MRSQUINNKELLY
INSTAGRAM.COM/RENEWYOUPODCAST

# Introduction

I know what you might be thinking:

*Here we are again. Another Christian lady writing about confidence like she's got it all figured out. She's got no idea what I've been through or what it's like to be me!*

I hear you, my friend. And I'll be the first to admit that 1) I don't have it all figured out; 2) I get how hard it is to feel confident when life repeatedly knocks you down; and 3) I understand how annoying it is to receive unsolicited advice from people who have never walked a day in your shoes.

But girl, let me just tell you something:

*This confidence devotional is different!*

It's hilarious, humbling, and hopeful all at the same time. It's designed to make you laugh, revamp your perspective, and allow you to see yourself the way Jesus does. It will help you to leave comparison behind for good—because after all, you don't need to become more like *her* when you're becoming more like *Him*!

Follow me on Instagram @hannahcrews.blog as we go on this journey of finding a confidence that changes everything. You are fearfully and wonderfully made—and P.S., you're cute when you smile, by the way!

*Hannah Crews*

# Purpose Like a Pineapple

*You shall be a crown of beauty
in the hand of the Lord,
and a royal diadem
in the hand of your God.*

ISAIAH 62:3 ESV

You might have noticed that there are pineapples drawn all over this book. I'm not necessarily a huge fruit lover, but if you place a freshly sliced pineapple in front of me—forget it. I will go absolutely feral. Uncontrollable, unrestricted, unladylike feral. Can you blame a girl, though? Pineapples are juicy and flavorful, and they have like a million health benefits. Sign me up, baby!

As I began the process of writing this devotional, I researched imagery that correlated to the topic of confidence. Pineapples popped up frequently, and I didn't know why, until one photo explained it with these words:

*"Stand tall, wear a crown, and be sweet on the inside."*

I let out a little gasp, because how darling is that analogy? Think about it: When you envision a pineapple, it stands tall on its own, perfectly postured with tropical charm. It's adorned with a leaflike crown on its head, displaying an effortlessly regal appearance. And famously, the golden fruit beneath its elegant surface is altogether aromatic, tender, and sweet.

As a beautiful daughter of the Most High God, you are destined to live with purpose like a pineapple. The day you accepted Jesus was the day you became royalty. He has set you apart, crowned you with confidence, and given you the main ingredient you need to stay sweet on the inside—the Word of God.

The Lord's perfect will for you is to live your life this way. He wants to see you stand tall, carrying yourself with radiant joy. He desires to see you embrace your unique calling, to fulfill it excellently with royal dignity. And most importantly, He longs to ripen your heart with Scriptures that will encourage you to turn from every bitter sin that tries to ferment your soul.

Be confident in this, my darling pineapple friend:

The more time you spend with Jesus, the sweeter you will become.

*Father, I long to live with purpose like a pineapple. Thank You for reminding me that You've adopted me into Your royal family. Help me to act and talk like it and treat others around me with Christlike sweetness. Amen.*

# Confidence vs. Self-Esteem

*Such confidence we have through Christ before God.*
II CORINTHIANS 3:4 NIV

Life sure is tough, isn't it? The things we go through shape everything about us—how we think, how we act, and how we see ourselves. We've experienced crazy things as kids, walked through bullying and breakups as teens, and are bombarded with mountains of pressure as adults. And to think, this world used to be *perfect*—but alas, sin crept in and ruined that. Honestly, if I ever run into Eve in heaven, I might or might not give her the stink eye and say, "Hey! Thanks a *lot*, Grandma!" But then I'd feel bad, because it's true—she is our grandma, guys. So, no, let's not do that.

Throughout the pages of this book, we'll learn how to find a confidence that changes everything. But before we get into the nitty-gritty, let's address some basic differences between self-esteem and self-confidence:

*Self-esteem* is how you view your value and worth.

*Self-confidence* is the attitude you have toward your abilities and skills.

Someone with *high self-esteem* knows how valuable and worthy they are as a child of the Most High God, but someone with *low self-esteem* questions if they're worthy or valuable at all. On the flip side, someone with *high self-confidence* knows they can do all things through Christ who gives them strength, but someone with *low self-confidence* doesn't believe their abilities and skills are "that great" at all.

Before we can even tackle the notion of finding confidence, we must address this self-esteem thing first. If you have ever questioned your value or your worth, or if you've ever been told you're invaluable and worthless, let me tell you the truth:

You were knit together with *love and intention* in your mother's womb.

Someone paid a horrific price for you, *just so you didn't have to.*

You've got a purpose that *no one*, and I mean *no one else,* can fulfill.

You have been accepted, forgiven, and adored *in the ways you've always longed for.*

According to Him, you are so valuable that you were worth dying for. Get ready to start seeing yourself the way Jesus sees you—it's going to bring you a confidence that changes everything!

> God, yes, I am valuable and worth it in Your sight—but help me see that every day of my life. Amen.

# Proceed with Confidence

*So we can confidently say, "The L*ORD *is my helper;
I will not fear; what can man do to me?"*

**HEBREWS 13:6 ESV**

By nature, I am a relatively cautious person. If pain occurs or if trust is compromised, I have a tendency to think twice before going down that road again. For example: If a curling iron melts my entire thumbprint off, I proceed with caution in the future. If a sketchy business promises me *FREE! FREE! FREE!* but fails to mention the *$TRING$* attached, I proceed with caution in the future. If a person treats me (or someone I love) like absolute dog doo-doo, I proceed with caution in the future. And transparently, sometimes my own caution tries to build an unhealthy fortress around the perimeters of my wounded heart. Consequently, I've had to grow cautious of my own caution! Which sounds funny, and it's quite a merry-go-round to explain, but maybe you get my drift.

I've encountered lots of cynical, pessimistic, and bitter people in my life—and all of them had a history of being burned. Unfortunately, it didn't happen to them overnight, and their grueling journey was far from pleasant.

But here's what's interesting: I've also encountered lots

of hopeful, optimistic, and joyful people in my life—and they had a history of being burned too! In fact, some of their burns were so bad, it made me wonder why they were still smiling.

However, the difference was clear: The person who embraced wholeness and healing, instead of staying tattered and torn, always chose Jesus. They chose to courageously proceed with confidence in the Lord as their helper rather than fearfully proceeding with caution against whatever could happen next.

Don't get me wrong, proceeding with caution is okay when rooted in wisdom and discernment. We live in a broken world, and painful circumstances are inevitable. However, we must not allow our caution to override our confidence in Christ. Here's the truth: No matter how badly we've been burned, Jesus will always work things out for our good. He will never break our trust, never cause us to stumble, and never lead us to make a mistake.

Proceed with confidence today. Pursue healing, embrace tenderness, and smile—because His plans for you are always good.

> God, I choose to proceed with confidence in You. Create in me a hopeful, optimistic, and joyful heart. Amen.

# Conviction: A Grace Warning

*And when He [the Holy Spirit] comes,
He will convict the world of its sin,
and of God's righteousness,
and of the coming judgment.*
**JOHN 16:8 NLT**

"Mom, I didn't get my initials today!" my kids exclaimed while grenade-launching their backpacks into my SUV. Instead of saying hello to me after school *(um, quite rude)*, these words about "initials" are usually the first to be shouted out of their PB&J-smeared mouths. Telling me that they successfully completed a school day without misbehaving is exciting to them.

Their teachers refer to initials as a "grace warning" *(which is so cute)*. However, further disobedience naturally leads to stronger chalkboard warnings—a full name, a checkmark, a double checkmark, and eventually. . .the principal's office. But the school's consistency of grace-based correction methods allows my children to value the importance of obedience and respect; and in turn, it boosts their confidence when they choose to do the right thing.

The Holy Spirit does this for us too. The moment we act in ways that are unbecoming, He gives us a "grace warning" in the form of conviction. These warnings may start with a gentle nudge, but when we continue to choose sin, stronger warnings occur. Eventually, our disobedience may result in tough consequences, but He only convicts us in ways that are meant for our good.

I have grown to love the Holy Spirit's conviction. Even when it's embarrassing or painful, conviction is proof that He sees me. He sees me as valuable enough to refine my character for His glory. He sees me as precious enough to redirect my life down a road of promises rather than pain. He sees me as capable enough to handle a greater purpose, as long as my heart remains aligned with His. His conviction gives me hope, and it boosts my confidence greatly.

Listen here: Conviction is a good thing, friend. Don't deny it. Don't run from it. Conviction doesn't mean you're altogether bad; it means that His plans for you are altogether good. Whether conviction comes in the form of wise counsel, Scripture, or His still, small voice—receive His conviction as a gift. He is pruning you to prepare you, and that is exciting!

*God, I love Your "grace warnings." Convict me in my sinfulness, so I can redirect and walk confidently in the call You have for my life. Amen.*

# "You Are Impressive"

*And let us consider
how we may spur one another
on toward love and good deeds.*
**HEBREWS 10:24 NIV**

Since I'm actually pretty introverted (shocker, but it's true), I've had to overcome the dread of outings that involve other humans. This includes things like volunteering as a parent chaperone for school field trips. Okay, wow, that sounds so awful as I type this out; I promise I'm not a deadbeat mom. But I'd be lying to you if I didn't admit that the idea of small talk with other parents for six whole hours comes with a hefty amount of preloaded exhaustion. I know, it sounds ridiculous. Or maybe you're cracking up because you know this invisible struggle all too well.

Recently, though, I put on my big girl panties and signed up to chaperone a museum field trip. This time, I prayed, "Lord, help me to feel energized and excited about this. Help me bless someone today."

Sure enough, the Lord placed two women in my path. One mom, a prominent business owner who juggles many hats, chose to chaperone while battling a tough day. The other mom, an involved and extremely present super-parent, chose to chaperone on her birthday. In their own unique and special ways, both women impressed me greatly. They showed me that even though they could've stayed home, they showed up anyway, despite their circumstances. After the trip was over, I sent them both individual text messages and included this simple phrase:

*"You are impressive."*

Oh, how certain words can drastically change the tone of a person's day. Both moms couldn't contain their gratitude, and in turn, the confidence I had in my God-given purpose skyrocketed that day too. When we choose to boost someone else's confidence, it overflows with a confidence boost within our own hearts too.

Our words have the power to bring life or death. Therefore, it is very important to choose our words wisely when speaking into the lives of others. Consider this:

Instead of breathlessly saying, "I don't know how you do it..." say, *"You are impressive."*

Instead of timidly saying, "I could never do what you do..." say, *"You are impressive."*

Instead of jokingly saying, "Look at you, overachiever..." say, *"You are impressive."*

If you're not feeling confident today, choose to edify someone anyway. I promise, it's a win-win!

> Lord, give me an opportunity to encourage someone today with my words. Amen.

# Anything You Can Do, I Can Do Better

*Therefore encourage one another
and build one another up...*
I THESSALONIANS 5:11 ESV

"Anything you can do, I can do better."

If you sang that out loud, you're my people. If you read it silently, are you okay and can I pray for you? *(Kidding!)*

If the concept of "one-upping" was a song, "Anything You Can Do" would be it. While this classic tune brings some laughs, it touches on a very real scenario in interpersonal relationships. One-upping happens when there is an air of competitiveness between two people, and in every case, it is driven by pride or insecurity.

In the Bible, John includes language that appears to one-up Peter at first glance. He refers to himself multiple times as "the disciple that Jesus loved," and even wrote about running faster than Peter to Jesus' tomb. Since I tend find the humor in most situations, I can't help but let out a little giggle when I read John's recollection of events. Now, there is no evidence that suggests John had a rift with Peter, and most Bible scholars don't believe there was any bad blood between the two disciples. But, both men were two of Jesus' top three besties, so who knows if there was some competition or not? John was human, after all!

Here's the deal, though. For us to walk confidently in our God-given identity, two things must happen:

1. One-upping comments must never leave our lips.
2. We must remain unbothered when others do it.

If you have a desire to one-up someone out of pride or insecurity, rebuke it right away. If someone speaks to you with a one-upping heart, pay no mind to it. Simply put—don't let the spirit of one-upping rule you in any way, shape, or form!

God has the ability to lift us up in ways we could never do for ourselves. He prefers that we have pure hearts and good intentions in every situation, especially in our interactions with others. Living this way breeds a God-like confidence and leads to more peaceful and fulfilling relationships within the body of Christ!

*God, help me to live pride- and- insecurity-free. May the words I say and the interactions I have with others be a good reflection of You. Amen.*

# Who Is God's Favorite?

*And remember that the heavenly Father to whom you pray has no favorites. He will judge or reward you according to what you do. So you must live in reverent fear of Him during your time here as "temporary residents."*

I PETER 1:17 NLT

My kids and I like to joke around with a silly game. It starts with this question: "Hey Mom, who is your favorite kid?"

"Hugh is my favorite!" I'll say, while my daughter displays a wide-mouthed reaction of dramatic horror. Or, "Lace is my favorite!" I'll say, while my son tightens his tough-guy lips and gives his sister a side-eye glare. After a brief pause, the three of us will erupt in obnoxious laughter. I end the game by saying, "Lace is my baby girl, and Hugh is my baby boy. You're both my favorite!"

My children love to know they're my favorite. However, they also know I don't *play* favorites. If they act out of line, I will correct them accordingly. If they display good character, I will reward them accordingly. They are equally loved, yet they are equally redirected when necessary.

Being that He is a good, good Father, God does the same with us. He doesn't *play* favorites, yet *you are* His favorite. You are fully known and loved by Him, and He handpicked you for an amazing purpose. At the same time, remember this: If *you're* His favorite, so is *she*. So is *he*. So am *I*. So is *everyone*. Therefore, it is important for us to think twice before acting (or reacting) against God's other kids. He sees every situation clearly, and He fairly rewards us or judges us when necessary. Living in awe of the Lord aligns our character with His, and He takes care of the rest.

What a wonderful feeling to know we are so loved. What confidence it brings knowing He will fight for us, defend us, and lift us up when we choose what is right. Yet, when we stumble, He will also correct us, redirect us, and refine us for His glory. I love that about Him. He is truly the perfect parent—I am His favorite, and so are you!

*God, You're my favorite. Thank You for your blessings and Your correction. Your love gives me a confidence that changes everything. Amen.*

# Ask the Hard Questions

*"Ask and it will be given to you;
seek and you will find;
knock and the door
will be opened to you."*
MATTHEW 7:7 NIV

During my first job as a news reporter, I was extremely green. With minimal experience and epically unfamiliar with the newsroom's software and equipment, I felt like a toddler trying to drive a car. The "dumb blonde" stereotype fit me perfectly, and I could tell my elementary-level questions were starting to irritate veteran coworkers. God forbid I be dubbed "the most annoying chick in the office," so I stopped asking questions altogether. But man, oh man, did that make things worse! Late nights, huge mistakes, and boatloads of tears later, my confidence was that of a skittish naked mole rat. I failed way more than I succeeded, and my reputation of cluelessness probably dubbed me "the most annoying chick in the office" anyway. Bless my heart.

Even though it was super cringe, I am so grateful for that experience. It taught me that confident people aren't afraid to ask hard questions. They don't care about looking stupid, bothering people, or assuming they know the answer. They ask people who are qualified, seek guidance without reserve, and research until they are fully secure on what to do next.

Here's the thing: *God* wants you to ask Him questions. Every painfully hard question, every seemingly ignorant question, even questions you've already asked a million times, He still wants you to ask. He will never make you feel like an idiot, never dismiss you for being "too much," never leave you hanging without providing an answer. He doesn't dread your questions, He looks forward to them! Even better, He will *definitely not* dub you as "the most annoying the chick in the office." What a relief!

Read Matthew 7:7 again. Jesus is serious when He says this. We can ask anything, and in due time, He will give us a "yes," "no," or "wait" answer. We can seek answers by researching the truth in His Word, and we will find it. We can knock, and He will open doors for us that no one else can.

Confidently ask your questions today. They are welcomed by a patient Father!

God, thank You for allowing me to ask You anything. It boosts my confidence knowing You'll guide me on what to do next. Amen.

# Leave the Past at the Well

*The woman left her water jar beside the well
and ran back to the village, telling everyone,
"Come see a man who told me everything I ever did!
Could He possibly be the Messiah?"*
JOHN 4:28-29 NLT

The Samaritan woman had a past. A lengthy one. Multiple husbands, loads of regret, and mistakes that more than likely *everyone* in her community knew about *(in full, embarrassing detail)*. Good thing social media wasn't around back then, because this chick's private life would have been more viral than a Kardashian's. It was so bad, poor thing chose to travel for water in the afternoon when it was too hot for others to go. She was so crippled by shame, it dictated her decision-making—even with basic daily chores.

But one divine afternoon, Jesus met her at the well. For this broken, guilt-ridden, used and abused girl—He went out of His way to see her. To look her in the eye. To tell her, before He told anyone else, Who He truly was: *The Messiah*. He removed her shame, gave her healing water, and wiped her past clean there at the well.

With no more desire to hide her face, the Samaritan woman ran back to her village and told everyone about Jesus.

Sometimes the mistakes we have made, or the traumas we have walked through, cause us to hide our faces in shame. They're too painful to deal with in private, let alone in public. If that's you today, I want to do something with you right now.

I want you to close your eyes and imagine yourself as the Samaritan woman.

Recall your burdens as you travel for water in the heat of day.

Think of your emptiness as you stare inside your dry, wooden bucket.

Feel your heaviness as you sit on a well built with ancient stone.

Now. . .look up.

Witness the tender face of Jesus.

Let Him gaze at your tear-filled eyes with His eyes of compassion.

Receive supernatural healing through His living water.

And leave your past at the well.

Our God is a restorer. Walk confidently today, sharing the goodness of Jesus with everyone you meet.

*God, thank You for seeing me.*
*Take my shame away for good. I choose*
*to leave my past at the well. Amen.*

# Triggered or Glimmered?

*"Until now you have asked nothing in my name. Ask, and you will receive, that your joy may be full."*
JOHN 16:24 ESV

I come from a family of skilled outdoorspeople. Deer season meant trips to west Texas, early mornings in a rackety old blind, and enough venison to feed our bellies for months. Vegetarians, you're really missing out on my grandma's stew, I'm just saying!

Being a hunter's granddaughter also meant learning how to safely use a rifle at a young age. However, shooting was never my favorite. It was loud, it was jolting—but what freaked me out the most was that dadgum trigger. My scrawny little fingers would barely touch it, and the kickback would throw me butt-first on the ground, covering my Limited Too glitter jeans with sticker burrs and fresh rabbit turds. So, yeah, I definitely preferred pulling up a wildflower over pulling back a trigger.

The word *trigger* has several different meanings. Therapists use it as a medical term—this is not the type of "trigger" we will be addressing here. No, in today's world, the word *trigger* describes a sensitive response from someone who is feeling on edge and may be seeking reasons to feel upset. In this sense of the word, you can touch someone's trigger, even on accident, and BOOM—you're met with an explosion. But here's the reality: Jesus doesn't want us to live on edge, He doesn't want us to live triggered, He wants us to live healed! He wants to bring stability in all areas of our lives—socially, relationally, professionally, but also spiritually, mentally, and emotionally. Because yes, if we actively look for a reason to be offended, we will find it. If we actively seek causation to be anxious or afraid, we will find it.

Instead of being trigger-focused, what if we became glimmer-focused instead? Noticing traces of kindness in people, marveling at a day of pretty weather, getting excited when we hit every green light, or *literally* stopping to smell the roses at the grocery store? There is power in acknowledging God's goodness, both great and small. Therefore, a glimmered life leads to a confident life! It causes our hearts to overflow with peace and our attitudes to exude with joy.

Live glimmered, girlfriend. His light shines so much brighter on your pretty little face when you do!

> **God, show me all the glimmers today. Living a triggered life doesn't serve me; heal me so I can joyfully, and confidently, serve You. Amen.**

There is power in acknowledging God's goodness, both great and small.

# Take Your Supplements!

*Supplement your faith with a generous provision of moral excellence, and moral excellence with knowledge, and knowledge with self-control, and self-control with patient endurance, and patient endurance with godliness, and godliness with brotherly affection, and brotherly affection with love for everyone.*
II PETER 1:5-7 NLT

My mom always made us take supplements growing up, and I loathed it. Chomping on multivitamins that tasted like sidewalk chalk or swallowing pills that made me burp straight acid was not fun. However, I did what any golden child would do—secretly flushed them right down the toilet.

Now that I'm a mom myself, I totally see the value of making my own kids take daily supplements—otherwise we'd be dealing regularly with midnight vomit sessions or weeks of walrus-sounding coughs. And sorry, I ain't about that life.

Another definition of *supplement* is "to add to." Webster defines *supplement* as "something that completes or enhances something else." Just like we have to take supplements to keep our bodies healthy, did you know that we have to take spiritual supplements to keep our faith healthy too? I never realized this until I opened up Second Peter chapter 1 and read about the seven key supplements we need to practice daily in order to grow in our walk with

Christ. They are:

1. *Moral excellence.* Displaying good character allows our lives to look more like Jesus.
2. *Knowledge.* Studying God's Word provides us with truth and facts that can help us effectively lead others to Christ.
3. *Self-control.* Fighting unhealthy desires leads to an overflow of blessings and favor.
4. *Patient endurance.* Giving grace and staying calm in the storm allows for a more peaceful life.
5. *Godliness.* Living with respect and genuine awareness of the Lord's goodness causes us to pursue a God-pleasing lifestyle.
6. *Mutual affection.* Friendship connects us as believers and helps us support each other in our faith, leading us toward a life well lived.
7. *Love.* This is God's greatest commandment. Being generous with our words, talents, charity, and affection is the best way to become the hands and feet of Jesus.

Being confident of who we are in Christ requires us to take daily spiritual supplements. Which one of these will you be adding to your faith walk today?

God, help me to add these supplements in my spiritual walk with You. Amen.

# The Pessimist, The Optimist, & The Psalmist

*Thou preparest a table before me in the presence of mine enemies; thou anointest my head with oil; my cup runneth over.*

**PSALM 23:5 KJV**

It's hard to walk in confidence when the world is crashing down on you. And if people are speaking against you in the process, forget it! Might as well crawl under a rock. Trust me, I know this feeling all too well. It's debilitating and soul-sucking and makes you wanna punch a Karen at the same time. *(Just kidding, don't do that. Like I said in my last book, I have an Aunt Karen. She's nice.)*

Sometimes the voices of opposition around us are so loud we can barely shower, let alone walk confidently into a room. But whenever I go through times like this, I have developed a very effective strategy. Before bed, I will open the book of Psalms and read it until it I fall asleep. I've done this for years, and it works every time. My heart floods with peace, depression gradually lifts off my shoulders, and a supernatural confidence starts to rise within me. God steps in and helps me face another day.

Some people are naturally positive through hardship, and others become cynical when life gets tough. But because we have the hope of Jesus, we can be another type of person:

Pessimist: "The glass is half empty."
Optimist: "The glass is half full."
Psalmist: "My cup runneth over."

I mean, come on. Somebody put that on a coffee cup, for crying out loud! *(Oh wait, we did! Grab one on Dayspring.com.)*

Psalmists walk in peace. They know that goodness and mercy will always follow them. They know that no matter what happens, good or bad, they will one day dwell in the house of the Lord forever. They have a heavenly mindset rather than an earthly one, an attitude of praise rather than an attitude of complaint. If that's not the definition of confidence, I don't know what is!

No matter what you're going through, be a psalmist. Even if it's not in your nature to see things like a psalmist would, you've got a Savior who can help. Read Psalms, watch God show up, and walk confidently knowing that He can restore your weary heart!

*God, I choose to be a psalmist today. Thank You for Your goodness and mercy. Amen.*

# You're a Failure. Not!

*No, in all these things
we are more than conquerors
through him who loved us.*

ROMANS 8:37 ESV

In the process of writing this devotional, I got a package in the mail. It was Becky Kiser's new hot-pink book, *But God Can: How to Stop Striving and Live Purposefully and Abundantly*. I impulsively yelled out, "Well, hot dog!" But right when I said that, I felt so cringe. I have no idea why, either. Maybe it was my tone? Maybe I added a foreign accent? Whatever it was, I immediately looked around to see if anyone heard me. Thankfully, no one did.

Anyway, back to the hot-pink book. One chapter was about all the lies we believe about ourselves that destroy our confidence. Things like "I'm not likeable. I'm fat. I'm ruining my kids. I'm not desirable enough for my husband..." You get the picture. Becky encourages us to pinpoint our "core lie," the one that shapes how we conduct ourselves. I prayed, "Lord, I don't know what my core lie is. Can you tell me?"

And boy, Jesus sure is precious with His responses! In His sweetness, in His gentleness, in His grace-laced voice, He tenderly revealed my core lie with three simple words:

"That you'll fail."

Those words, while normally gut-punching, didn't rock me at all—because of the way He said it. He spoke in such a nonchalant, trivial, no-big-deal way—kind of like when a daddy smiles and ensures his weeping child that there are no monsters under the bed. I let out a sigh of relief, saying, "Yes, Lord, that's it."

Maybe you, too, know what it's like to have "failphobia." *(Not a word. Made that up. But it sounds good.)* Maybe you are terrified of failing people if you don't excel scholastically or professionally. Maybe you are terrified of ending up like a "Jane Doe" who meaninglessly coasts through life and dies unknown and insignificant. Maybe you are terrified of being unloved, just a beat-up loser with no one in your corner of the boxing arena.

But guess what? God doesn't say we're failures—He says we're more than conquerors! He doesn't say our lives hold little meaning—He says our lives have great purpose! He doesn't say we're unloved—He says His love *never fails*!

Close your eyes and allow Jesus to fill you with the same relief He gave me.

> God, thank You
> for never failing me. Amen.

# Level Up!

*One's pride will bring him low,
but he who is lowly in spirit will obtain honor.*
**PROVERBS 29:23 ESV**

It is easy to identify ourselves with the heroes of the Bible. But sometimes, whether we like it or not, our sinful nature can be identified in the Bible's villains too. Case in point—King Nebuchadnezzar. He's the dude who threw three young men—Shadrach, Meshach, and Abednego—into the fiery furnace because they refused to worship a golden statue. Very rude of him, I know; thankfully, the story ends extremely well. They emerged from the flames unharmed due to God's protection.

Yes, King Nebby was a haughty man, a stubborn man, a man who idolized himself more than he honored God. His pride eventually led to dire consequences, where he literally went crazy and started eating grass like a cow *(not even joking)*. However, here's the cool part: After recognizing God's authority, King Nebsters humbled himself and praised God for His greatness. God then restored his life and promoted him to a higher level of influence than ever before.

Now, you might be thinking, *First of all, I've never thrown anyone into a fire. Second of all, King Nebz was doing too much. No way am I as prideful as that guy!* However, hear me out: pride is pride, and it presents itself differently in everyone. Some levels of pride are obvious—like King Nebman's grandiose golden statue of himself. Other levels of pride are subtle—like justifying a mistake by finger-pointing, making excuses for poor decisions, dismissing a sin as "not that bad," or holding on to plain old unforgiveness.

If we want a closer relationship with Christ, we must pass the "pride test" we're in right now. It's like school: once we pass first grade, we can move on to second grade, but if we fail, we'll be held back. Failing to release our pride will hold us back, leaving us stuck on a merry-go-round of repeated patterns and recycled problems. But there is hope! God, in His mercy, allows us opportunities to retake every test. Once we pass with a humble heart, we can victoriously move on to the next level with Him.

Today, let's pinpoint the pride in our lives (both obvious and subtle) and pray this prayer together:

> God, I'm sorry for the pride
> that has held me back.
> Humble my heart and show me
> how to make things right.
> I want to level up with You. Amen.

# God? Is That You?

*Eli realized it was the Lord
who was calling the boy.
So he said to Samuel, "Go and lie down again,
and if someone calls again, say,
'Speak, Lord, your servant is listening.'"*

I SAMUEL 3:8-9 NLT

Now that I've been married for a while, I can easily detect my husband's presence. If he walks down a hallway, I know it's him by the way he rhythmically thuds his heels against the floor. If I'm in a crowd, my spidey senses can quickly identify him by the echo of his deep, boisterous voice. If I wake up frightened after a comatose-like sleep, the cadence of his breathing lets me know that I, indeed, have *not* been kidnapped. Since I know him so well, my husband's presence feels like home to me.

In the Bible, Samuel didn't recognize God's voice. However, because of Eli's wise counsel, Samuel learned to discern when God was speaking and got to know Him well.

How can we confidently hear God's voice for ourselves? How can we know if it's Him speaking or if it's our own thoughts, emotions, and opinions? We can do this by:

1. *Studying Scripture.* The Bible is, literally, God talking to us. His Word tells us how to act, think, and live.

Scripture also renews our minds—and when our minds are renewed, hearing His voice becomes easier.
2. *A submissive heart.* To discern the voice of the Holy Spirit, we must be open to God's guidance. Otherwise, our pride will lead us to mistakes! Many times, God speaks to us through our conscience, both while we're awake and asleep.
3. *Godly influences.* Find an Eli in your life—a pastor, Christian counselor, or faithful mentor. These people will minister to you wisely, lead you constructively, and always point you to Jesus.

God wants to speak to you. He wants you to clearly recognize His voice. Why? Because you are His daughter! The more time you spend with Him, the more His presence feels like home.

*Lord, I want to hear Your voice clearly. Give me an Eli in my life. Lead me through Your written Word. I want my decisions to align with Your perfect will. Amen.*

# Comparison Kills Confidence

*A heart at peace gives life to the body,*
*but envy rots the bones.*

**PROVERBS 14:30 NIV**

Growing up, there were two Hannah L's in my class *(one of them was me, since my maiden name is Linn)*. But that other Hannah L, though. . . man, she was cool. So sweet, so respectful, so soft-spoken *(unlike me, the loudmouthed howler monkey)*. But also, Hannah L was a *total beast* at sports. Y'all don't even know—that chick was the legendary one on the team. She had a physique like a legendary athlete, shot hoops like a legendary baller, and ran track like a legendary sprinter. On the other hand, little old me bee-bopped around like a cricket on crack and mainly competed because it was fun. But, if we're being honest, it was fun because we won—like, all the time—largely thanks to Hannah L. Her presence made us winners too.

Unfortunately, girls like my friend Hannah L are easy targets for comparison. Flawed hearts see women like her through eyes of inferiority—brewing jealousy and killing confidence. And sadly, I see this happen among women within the body of Christ all the time.

In her book *Not from God,* Kaitlin Chappell Rogers

illustrates the tie between comparison and jealousy perfectly:

> *Comparison and Jealousy are like twin sisters. Comparison tells you to put your life up against someone else's, and Jealousy comes along and tells you to envy what they have.*
>
> *Comparison says you're [not as cool] as her, and Jealousy tells you to pick her apart to make yourself feel better.*

Because I love you, I'm going to give it to you straight: Comparison shifts a God-focused heart to a self-centered heart. Comparison swings the pendulum from inspiration to subtle hatred. It blinds the truth, rots the soul, and drives people to do things like gossip, manipulate, and inflict harm upon others and themselves.

Overcoming comparison buys us a one-way ticket to Confidence City, USA—with Jesus as the pilot! He flies us straight to destinations of contentment, joy, and gratefulness. He reveals to us that if His goodness is for her, it's for us too! When we love the Hannah L's in our life like Jesus does, we always remain on the winning team.

God, give me eyes to see Your goodness
in the women I admire. May it lead me
to a fulfilled, confident life. Amen.

# You Gifted Girl, You!

*As each has received a gift,*
*use it to serve one another,*
*as good stewards of God's varied grace.*
I PETER 4:10 ESV

Okay, I hope you're not too mad at me after yesterday's devotion! Please don't launch rotten tomatoes at me yet. *(Speaking of, I probably have some in my refrigerator right now. Yuck. That bottom drawer is basically a coffin for vegetables, don't you agree?)*

We talked about comparison. We discussed how it can hinder God's best for our lives. We brought up some convicting stuff—but, friend, I want to encourage you with this truth today:

*You are **extremely** gifted.*

If that statement made you snort with sarcasm, well, get ready for some exciting facts, sister!

The Bible makes it very clear that everyone is gifted. Yes, everyone. And God finds immeasurable value in each gift, equally. If God thinks our gifts are great, who are we to say they aren't? Every gift, obvious or subtle, is needed within the body of Christ. In Romans 12:6-8 (NLT), it says this:

*In His grace, God has given us different gifts for doing certain things well. So if God has given you the ability to prophesy, speak out with as much faith as God has given you. If your gift is serving others, serve them well. If you are a teacher, teach well. If your gift is to encourage others, be encouraging. If it is giving, give generously. If God has given you leadership ability, take the responsibility seriously. And if you have a gift for showing kindness to others, do it gladly.*

So often it's the "behind the scenes" gifts that have blessed me the most. The elderly woman who held the door open as I wrangled feisty babies. The stranger who asked to pray over me without knowing my heart was crushed. The teacher who said, "God is going to use you mightily!" so many times that I actually believed her.

Our gifts are not for us—they're for His glory. He gives us gifts so His Name can be magnified through our lives. Whatever that gift looks like for you, use it confidently. He has entrusted you with a world-changing assignment that no one else can fill.

God, thank You for the gifts You have given me. Show me how to steward them well and use them for Your glory. Amen.

# Created in His Image

*I will praise You,
for I am fearfully and wonderfully made.*
PSALM 139:14 NKJV

Body image. You knew it was coming, didn't you? I can't write a devotional about confidence without bringing this one up! We're women—we think about it, so we must talk about it!

I'm not too proud to admit I've allowed surface-level insecurities to determine my plans or dictate my actions. Things like wearing a sundress instead of a swimsuit because my body wasn't "summer ready." Or staying home from a night out because my outfits looked "frumpy." Or *(gasp)* whitening my coffee-stained teeth in a photo editing app.

Whether you've been guilty of these things or not, all of us have something about our bodies that we consider subpar. We see ourselves in the mirror and think, *God, You really could've done a better job on that one*. However, one day I read a quote that changed everything. It said:

*"Your body is the least interesting thing about you."*

What a perspective shift! I could physically feel certain insecurities within me start to dissipate. Sure, if my nostrils were a bra size, they'd be considered a DD, but it no longer bothers me. Sure, I grow a random patch of hair on my Adam's apple, but that's what razors are for. Sure, one of my eyes is lazier than the other, but I still have the gift of good vision.

When it comes to eternity, it's the heart that God values the most. While yes, it's totally okay to enhance one's natural beauty, our outward appearance is not what people will remember us by when we're gone. Instead, we will be remembered by the composition of our character. When we die, people more than likely won't say things like:

"Man, her lack of pimples really drew me closer to the Lord!"

"Wow, because of her zero-cellulite body, I started reading the Bible!"

"It's true, her wrinkle-free forehead caused me to rethink my faith!"

We've got to start seeing ourselves the way Jesus does. When we do, we live differently. Thank Him for creating you in His image—fearfully, wonderfully—and walk confidently in the amazing purpose He has for your precious life!

*God, thank You for creating me. Keep my heart pure, and help me to see myself (and all of my features) the way You do. Amen.*

# The Gift of Exercise

*Beloved, I pray that all may go well
with you and that you may be in good health,
as it goes well with your soul.*

III JOHN 1:2 ESV

"*Oh no, I don't do cardio.*" That line in *Pitch Perfect* is so hilarious, so relatable to me. Because honestly, sometimes even the sight of a treadmill provokes my heart to thump uncontrollably as beads of sweat simultaneously seep out of my semi-shaved pit pores.

Yes, it's true that the composition of our bodies is the least interesting thing about us. An average-shaped woman who is selfless, joyful, and purehearted is always more attractive than a fit chick who is self-absorbed, rude, and ill-intentioned.

*But...(yes, there's a "but!" Before you start gagging, let me remind you that this is a confidence devotional, after all!)* If we want to walk confidently with who we are in Christ, we must be willing to utilize every gift He has given us, including the ability to move our bodies! Exercise, indeed, is a gift—one we have all been given.

God was very intentional when He designed our bodies. It's a proven fact: consistent movement boosts one's confidence in a dramatic way, while consistent couch-sitting does the opposite. Not only does exercise produce good physical health, it improves our mental state thanks to *endorphins*. These hormones are released during a good workout, resulting in reduced stress and better moods. And let's face it, when our physical and mental states are healthier, that causes greater levels of confidence to spill over into other areas of life!

Even though we sometimes associate exercise with dread and pain, we must be intentional to reframe our thoughts about this. What if we started viewing exercise as a form of worship—thanking God for the ability to move, glorifying Him by stewarding our bodies well, singing His praises with Christian playlists as we work out?

I'm not expecting you to become a D1 athlete by tomorrow. But I am encouraging you to carve out thirty minutes a day to move your body in a way that is fun for you. Whether it's dancing with friends, walking in nature, or lifting fancy equipment—cherish your gift. Steward your body well. And give the Lord praise the entire time!

> God, thank You for this gift.
> I choose to be grateful as I exercise
> and treat my body well. Amen.

# A Confidence of Many Colors

*But his brothers hated Joseph*
*because their father loved him*
*more than the rest of them.*
*They couldn't say a kind word to him.*
**GENESIS 37:4 NLT**

Joseph was the favorite child, always had the finest gifts from daddy, and his brothers *hated him* for it. I always wondered why Joseph thought it was a smart idea to tell his brothers about "the dream"—you know, the one where they all bowed down to him? Like, come on Broseph. You really thought that would go over well? Take a hint, bud.

Joseph was unusually favored, which led to unusual suffering. Because he was loved the most, Joseph's brothers threw him into a pit and sold him into slavery. Because he looked like an Abercrombie model, Potiphar's wife desperately wanted Joseph's bod *(but he refused)*, so she falsely accused him of rape. Because he didn't compromise his integrity, Joseph was jailed and beaten and abandoned and forgotten.

It's hard to feel confident when you're surrounded by haters, especially when they intentionally try to harm you. But here's what I love about Joseph: Despite what others said about him, he held on to what was true and remained in perfect peace. Despite what people did to him, he endured every trial with perseverance and grace. Despite every unfair circumstance, he rested assured that God would pull through in a miraculous way.

Just like his coat of many colors, Joseph wore a confidence of many colors. The tapestry of his character was beautiful because of his unwavering faith. He knew that eventually God would rescue him from every hateful snare. However, the most valuable thing to note is Joseph's disposition:

He didn't walk in bitterness, self-pity, or unforgiveness.

He didn't waste any time plotting his revenge.

And more importantly, he didn't allow pride to take over. When he experienced success, giving a "shout-out to all the haters" was never on his radar.

Joseph's strategy was simple: trust God, have integrity, show mercy. That was it! If that's not confidence, I don't know what is! If we have this kind of character, one that resembles the heart of Jesus, God will always work things out for our good.

> Lord, people can be so hateful.
> But keep my character pure despite
> my pain. I want Your goodness to
> always shine through me. Amen.

Trust God,
have integrity,
&
show mercy.

# Praise Changes Things

*I will be glad and rejoice in Your unfailing love,*
*for You have seen my troubles,*
*and You care about the anguish of my soul.*

PSALM 31:7 NLT

In high school, there were days where I was so broken and crushed, all I wanted to do was skip school and go to my aunt Ann's house. I'd open the back door, unannounced, and she'd greet me with a "Hello, darlin'!" in her joyful elderly voice. Tearfully collapsing on her 1970s laminate floor, I'd woefully express my problems in teenage slang that she probably didn't understand. But as she sat in her pink suede recliner, with wrinkled eyes filled with cataracts and compassion, she would always say:

"Well, praise the Lord!"

I never understood it. Like, what was so praiseworthy about that, Annie Lee? I'd get over my annoyance quickly, though. Mainly because she'd offer me a cold glass of dark chocolate Ensure. *(Yes, I love old-people drinks, I really do.)*

What Aunt Ann understood, though, was the power of praise. And as I've grown in the things of the Lord, I'm understanding it too.

Let's be real—when times are tough, praising God isn't something we want to do. It feels unnatural. We'd rather plead with God, question God, beg Him to make things better. Praise, however, is the purest form of prayer. It shifts the focus off ourselves and onto Him. And here's what happens when we do:

- **Praise draws Him close.** When we exalt Him, thank Him, glorify Him—His Spirit shows up. God always abides and dwells within sounds of praise.
- **Praise makes us feel better.** It's a fact—praise brings us peace within chaos and relief from despair, allowing us to physically feel better. *(Why? Because, again, praise draws Him close!)*
- **Praise causes things to change.** Not only within us but around us—hearts change, attitudes change, minds change, situations change, and people change—all because of our praise.

Maybe it's not confidence we lack—maybe it's praise we lack. When things go south, when insecurity tries to creep in, when life gets overwhelming—let's start shouting, "Well, praise the Lord!" instead. Praise truly changes things—and it brings us a confidence that changes things too.

> Lord, I praise You. You're good, majestic, and powerful, and You love me. Thank You for showing up for me today as I praise Your Name. Amen.

# When Our Bodies Fail

*So we are always confident,
even though we know that
as long as we live in these bodies
we are not at home with the Lord.*

II CORINTHIANS 5:6 NLT

Do you ever have recurring nightmares of being chased, but you simply cannot move your legs fast enough? Same. I'm only capable of running in slow motion when a scary monster is barreling toward me *(even though the monster is always something random, like "Big Bird in a pair of overalls wielding a machete" random)*. And when I try to shout for help, forget it—all that comes out is a weak whisper-scream. In those nightmares, my body always fails me—leaving me scared, hopeless, and defeated.

Obviously, it's always a good idea to exercise regularly, eat healthy, and take care of ourselves. But even when we do all the right things, sometimes our bodies don't cooperate. We get injured, we get sick, or worse—and the feelings of being scared, hopeless, and defeated are no longer a dream—they're real life. How can we walk in confidence when our bodies are mangled, miserable, or withering away?

Sometimes we are guilty of taking our diagnosis and

centralizing an identity around it. We tend to label ourselves by our disease, condition, or disability because it's part of our everyday reality. But Second Corinthians 5 brings a new perspective on this. Paul emphasizes that we are to remain confident in the things of the Lord, despite our physical state. He reminds us that our bodily suffering is only a momentary affliction preparing us for eternal glory. He reassures us that no matter our condition, we are to always please God and do good for others while we're still here.

Sweet friend, your identity isn't attached to how pristine (or un-pristine) your health is. You're not a car, you know? You don't decrease in value once you're driven off the lot! You are just as needed for the kingdom of God when you're healthy as you are when you're not.

Next time the monster of fear, self-pity, or hopelessness tries to chase you down, plant your feet firmly in praise. Shout unto God with a voice of triumph, and do so with confidence until your very last breath!

> Lord, thank You for using me
> even when my body fails. I choose
> to live for You joyfully, confidently,
> and with purpose! Amen.

# Miss Dependent

*"I am the vine, you are the branches.
If you remain in Me and I in you,
you will bear much fruit;
apart from Me you can do nothing."*

JOHN 15:5 NIV

When the Barbie movie came out, it was highly controversial *(shocker, but hey, controversy seems to be this generation's middle name)*. One day on a plane ride home, Blaine and I decided to watch it to pass the time—and let me just say, the film taught me a huge lesson. Hold on, don't worry, I'm not here to praise the movie nor am I here to bash it! We've got much bigger fish to fry in today's devotion, girlfriend!

An overarching theme in the Barbie movie was independence. Independence as women, independence from societal norms, independence by living carefree from the opinions of others. Confidence exuded from Barbie: a glamorous, blissful, attractive confidence. The movie kinda made me want to see how much money I could get from my preserved, still-in-the-box vintage Barbie collection on eBay. But it also made me think, *Man, no amount of "girl-power independence" could ever make me not need Jesus!* Because personally, it's not *independence* that grows my confidence; my confidence grows when I walk *in dependence!*

The world tries to glorify independence and make it synonymous with confidence. But take another peek at today's verse: it ends by saying, "Apart from [Jesus] you can do nothing." What a striking phrase—one that humbles us enough to realize that hey, we ain't diddly-squat without our Savior! But also, what a comforting phrase—one that reminds us that we don't have to figure everything out on our own, because He already has everything figured out *(cue the sigh of relief)*!

One way to walk confidently and dependently on God is through our worship. Singing His praises and offering up our hearts in prayer keeps us focused on Christ, redirecting the attention away from ourselves and onto Him. It reminds us that His power is made perfect in our weakness, and it encourages us to surrender. Because let's face it—without Him, we'd fall flat on our heinies!

Have a worshipful attitude today. No matter how capable you are, dependence on God leads to more confidence than you can ever imagine!

> God, I choose to walk dependently on You. You've got it under control, and that fills me with confidence. Amen.

# The Domino Effect

*Sow your seed in the morning,
and at evening let your hands not be idle,
for you do not know which will succeed,
whether this or that, or whether
both will do equally well.*

**ECCLESIASTES 11:6 NIV**

Mornings are hard for me. Not because of any other reason other than I genuinely love sleep so much. If it were up to me, I'd sleep until noon every single day! It's a lazy yet extremely impressive quality, I know. You probably read that fun fact and thought, *Wow, how old are you? A teenager? Don't you think it's time to grow up?* And the answer is probably yes. But hey, the Bible says I'm a child of God, not an adult of God, alright? Just let me live!

I totally understand how even people who love to sleep must function responsibly in society. And as I've matured, I've noticed the value of starting each morning with at least one good choice. Waking up early always provides a small feeling of accomplishment, which leads to accomplishing other things, like making the bed, spending time with God, eating nutritious foods, getting in a good workout, finishing the to-do list, and enjoying a restful evening. It's a domino effect of good decisions; a satisfying experience as you watch each "good decision domino" successfully fall to its completion. Naturally, this causes you to end the day with a feeling of—*you guessed it*—confidence!

The domino effect of sowing good seeds in the morning, as it says in Ecclesiastes, is so important for us to embrace. But let's remember, the domino effect can go both ways—it happens when we make not-so-good decisions too. Sleeping the day away leads to a messy room, zero time for Bible reading, drive-thru meals, and procrastinating everything else on our to-do list due to overwhelm and emotional exhaustion.

Don't worry, there's grace! I've walked through those "meh" days a million times too. But, like you, I desire to walk in confidence. I want the domino effect of my day to begin and end with good decisions, leading to an abundant life!

> God, I want to have the right kind of domino effect today. Help me to remember how confident I feel when I make good choices. May my actions today be a reflection of You. Amen.

# Become a Student

*Do not conform to the pattern of this world,
but be transformed by the renewing of your mind.*
ROMANS 12:2 NIV

My husband knows to never put me in situations where I'm responsible for something I know nothing about. Like asking the CPA to explain our taxes *(I'm blonde, remember?)*, or doing a home improvement project *(I can barely hold a steak knife properly)*, or fixing a car with smoke billowing from the engine *(sorry bud, I'm not Megan Fox)*. Unfortunately, I'm about as useless as a limp fish in every single one of those situations.

It's easy for us to believe that if we don't *feel* confident about something, then we must be incapable. If we don't *feel* good enough, we never will be. While our feelings can be powerful, they don't always reflect reality. Don't get me wrong, emotions can guide us, helping us recognize areas for growth and encouraging us to push beyond our comfort zones. They play an important role in our lives, but if we're not careful, they can also lead us in the wrong direction.

The world suggests that confidence is a feeling, something we feel in our hearts about ourselves and our capabilities. However, that's not true at all! Confidence doesn't come from the heart; actually, it starts within the mind!

Let me explain. First, it's our thoughts that affect our feelings—not the other way around. To have a more confident heart, we must exercise our mind. For example, how did we pass that test in school? We actively learned about that subject. How did we become so passionate about our favorite hobby or trade? We actively learned about it. How did we fall more in love with our spouse, our friends, our Savior? By actively learning more about them.

If you're reading this devotional because you're tired of being insecure, or if you're just desperately wanting to know God more, the starting point is simple—*become a student*. The Bible is the perfect textbook. When we actively put our minds on learn mode, our perceptions start to filter out the lies and infiltrate our thoughts with the purity of God's truth instead.

The heart cannot love what the mind does not know; therefore, knowledge of our precious Savior is what we must chase after the most. Knowing the truth about who Jesus is, and who we are in Him, leads to a confidence that changes everything.

> God, knowing You is what I'm after.
> I pray my hunger for You is never
> satisfied. I want to be a student of who
> You are all the days of my life. Amen.

# Look at This Photograph

*I remember the days of old;*
*I meditate on all that you have done;*
*I ponder the work of your hands.*

**PSALM 143:5 ESV**

"Definitely not posting that one!" we say, after a random stranger takes a badly angled photo on our extremely cracked iPhone. "Girl, delete this!" we type, after being tagged in a picture in which our face looks like a proper troll. And don't even get me started with the throwbacks! Sometimes we think, *Man, I wish I was as "fat" right now as I thought I was* back *then!* Or, on a heavier note, we think, *Man, I wish I could just erase that memory out of my life completely.*

Photos have a funny way of either boosting our confidence or destroying it. Our eyes send a message to our minds, our minds then shape a perspective, and that perspective settles into our hearts.

But what if we started taking the Psalm 143:5 approach? Instead of looking at pictures (both present and past) with self-loathing, shame, or pain, let's do these three things:

1. *Reflect on the Lord's goodness.* Sure, that person might've been a toxic friend. But God later

surrounded you with kindhearted people. Sure, that body of yours might've been sixty pounds overweight. But what a gift it was to finally hold your newborn baby.
2. *Learn and grow from it.* God is a God of hope and of second chances. Photo memories of unhealthy habits or lifestyles can encourage us by reminding us of how far we've come, leading us to make wiser decisions for a godly future.
3. *Praise Him for what He's still doing.* God wants us to look at every photo and believe that the best is still yet to come. He will never stop pursuing us, refining us, and leading us. The images you take today will remind your future self that because He pulled through for you then, He will do it again.

Girl, take those pictures. No matter how uncomfortable it feels, documenting your precious life is a gift—a reminder that God was faithful then, is faithful now, and will be faithful forevermore!

*(Side note: Sorry if "Photograph" by Nickelback is playing relentlessly in your head. I couldn't help it. Hopefully you can replace it with some Jesus songs later.)*

> God, I choose the Psalm 143:5
> approach with every image
> I take and see. Amen.

# Be a Girl's Girl

*A man that hath friends
must shew himself friendly.*
PROVERBS 18:24 KJV

Trashy television always has a way of exposing the most unhinged sides of human nature. We watch it and think, *Wow, apparently I'm not as crazy as I thought I was!* While my reality TV consumption has decreased since my age has increased (and hopefully my maturity levels have too), sometimes I can't help but get sucked into a random episode while mindlessly flipping through channels on a Saturday night.

I once stumbled upon an episode where two girls were viciously arguing *(gasp, wait, girl drama? Shocker!)* One of the girls then shouted to the other, "You're not a girl's girl, and that's your problem!"

A "girl's girl?" I had never heard of that term before. But it intrigued me, so I did some good ol' Google research and came up with this cumulative definition:

**Girl's girl (n):** *a woman who respects female friendships and supports the success of other women. Refuses to allow jealousy, drama, or other petty behaviors come between them. Values kindness, courtesy, loyalty, and unconditional love above all else.*

A "girl's girl" runs from comparison like the plague. She is secure, complimentary, kindhearted, and selfless. Seeing other women flourish is never a threat to her own worth, and she finds joy in championing other women no matter how chaotic or messy her own life can be.

If we want to experience confidence within our female friendships, we must first be a "girl's girl" ourselves. This certainly doesn't mean we have to like "girly" things, like makeup or shopping—it simply means we are safe enough for other women to trust us, connect with us, and enjoy being around us.

A "girl's girl" closely aligns with what the Bible says about friendship. For us to *have* good friends, we must *be* a good friend.

Find a way to be a "girl's girl" today. Go out of your way to champion someone you admire, serve someone you adore, or display the kind of love that Jesus would— without expecting anything in return. Building a foundation of good character will definitely lead to strong, meaningful relationships!

> God, I want to have confidence
> in the area of female friendships.
> Help me to be a "girl's girl," and place
> godly women in my path who will
> be a good friend to me too. Amen.

# Praying with Confidence

*And this is the confidence that we have toward him,*
*that if we ask anything according to his will he hears us.*
I JOHN 5:14 ESV

It's no secret that I'm a huge fan of laughing. Receiving good doses of joy in a clean, wholesome way is a huge part of my life. Therefore, I follow a lot of Christian humor accounts on Instagram. There's one viral video that gets me every time: a gentle-hearted pastor who starts off his normal Sunday morning sermon by addressing his congregation like this:

*"Let us pray. Heavenly farts, I mean. . .(quickly catches himself). . . Heavenly Father, we come before You today. . ."*

Bless his heart, that pastor did not intend to get so tongue-tied. But that innocent mistake has given millions of people around the world a good elementary-school-style chuckle.

Maybe praying out loud causes you to freeze up. If finding the confidence to speak to God verbally is something you struggle with, let me encourage you with this: God never cringes when you pray!

Think about it this way. When a toddler speaks lovingly toward you, even if they get their words slightly mixed up, does it make you cringe? No! The same goes for your heavenly Father. As today's verse reminds us, we can be confident that if we ask *anything* according to His will, He will hear us—even if we stumble over our words a little bit.

If praying is still awkward for you, though, try using the *P.A.R.T.* method:

*Praise.* Give God glory for who He is and what He's done in your life.

*Admit.* Apologize for the things that are not pleasing to Him.

*Request.* Ask for forgiveness, for Him to provide, for Him to reveal Himself to you.

*Thank.* Verbalize your gratitude for all He has done and will do in the future.

Psalm 23, The Lord's Prayer, gives us a beautiful example of this as well. Remember, prayer is simply a conversation with Jesus—kind of like one you'd have with your bestie. All He wants is a relationship with you, and relationships form through talking to each other. Speak to Him, and let Him speak to you!

*God, I desire to pray confidently. Remove my fear of what others think. Let me praise You, admit things to You, request things of You, and thank You with my whole heart. Amen.*

# Discernment Boosts Confidence

*The one who gets wisdom loves life;*
*the one who cherishes understanding*
*will soon prosper.*

**PROVERBS 19:8 NIV**

Siri is the best, especially when it comes to navigation. Girlfriend just knows! She tells us where to go, how to avoid stuff, and gets us to our destination in the most successful way possible. This is great for someone like me who has trouble knowing my right hand from my left *(not even kidding)*. Siri provides insights, or a discernment in direction, that I simply don't have—and because of her direction, I'm confident that I'll get to where I'm going without any hiccups.

Discernment is mentioned a lot in the Bible. It's the ability to perceive and understand things clearly—properly distinguishing between what's right and wrong, what's good and bad. Discernment is also 100 percent from God. The Holy Spirit prompts us to do what is right, and He will *never* lead us astray. Spiritually mature discernment allows us to decipher between what our human desires want and what God wants. It's God's way of showing us how things really are, instead of how we want them to be.

Discernment is also important when adhering to the voices of influence around us. Our circle matters—listening to people with a track record of wisdom and successful outcomes is much better than listening to people with a history of ignorance and poor choices. We must be careful to not surround ourselves with "yes people" who affirm everything we say and do. Instead, we must include "no people" in our circle too—ones who love us enough to boldly say something before we take a disastrous turn.

The most confident people I've ever met are people with high levels of discernment. They show no signs of insecurity because discernment has given them a prosperous life—in relationships, in finances, and in ministry. Discernment leads to confidence, one that changes everything—because this kind of confidence doesn't come from self-love, it comes from chasing after God.

Discernment prevents us from experiencing a life of pain and provides us with a life of peace. Walking in discernment, in word and in deed, will change everything for the better!

> God, I invite Your discernment into my life. I want less of me in my thoughts and decisions, and more of You. Have Your way, and fill me with Your Spirit. Amen.

# The Most Important Devotion You'll Ever Read

*I am the way, the truth, and the life.
No one can come to the Father
except through Me.*
JOHN 14:6 NLT

Look at you! You've completed thirty days of growing more confident in who you are in Christ—pretty cool, friend. Pretty cool.

If you're new here, we do something together at the end of each thirty-day period. Just like in my book *Goodness Gracious: 90 Unfiltered Devotions for this Sometimes-too-Serious Life*, I extend an opportunity for you to surrender your life to Jesus. You might be like, *Whoa, I don't think I'm ready for that yet.* Or you might think, *I can go ahead and skip this devotion then.* But don't do that, goofy! This might be the most important devotion you'll ever read!

Let's face it: life is short. We might consider ourselves young right now—but if we die tomorrow, we're actually pretty old if you think about it. Since we don't know when our time will end, it's important that we don't waste any time at all—and choose today to surrender our hearts to Jesus.

Here's the truth: If we want to get to heaven one day,

following Jesus is *the* way, not *a* way. All other ways, truths, and lifestyles will result in sorrow, confusion, and an eternity separated from His glory. Accepting Jesus as our Lord and Savior not only gives us the promise of eternal life, it also allows us to live a purpose-filled life while we're still here.

If you've ever questioned your salvation, if you're unsure if heaven is where you'll end up, or if you feel like you've fallen away from Him—today is the day, friend. The Bible says if we confess with our mouths that Jesus is Lord and believe in our hearts that God raised Him from the dead (Romans 10:9), we will be saved. He has been calling you, and now is the time to answer!

Pray this prayer out loud with me:

> Jesus, I'm done wasting time. I surrender my life to You. I believe that Your death paid for my mistakes and that You came back to life, showing me that I can have hope and a new beginning in You. I trust that You are with God in heaven and that You have a plan for me. Today, I fully open my heart to You. Amen.

Wow. Praise God. I'm proud to call you family!

Accepting Jesus as our Lord and Savior not only gives us the promise of eternal life, it also allows us to live a purpose-filled life while we're still here.

# Open and Closed Doors

*What He opens, no one can close;
and what He closes, no one can open.*
REVELATION 3:7 NLT

My oldest brother, Christopher, is known for his "man cave." Well, actually, it's just his garage; but this ain't no ordinary garage, folks. It has high-definition television screens, a full-sized dining table, and a ridiculously decked-out refreshment center. But is there any room for, let's say, *his truck*? Absolutely not! Placing cars in a garage is both silly and impractical in my brother's world—who does that?

Christopher's garage, though, is the place where meaningful memories are made. It's where he met both of my babies, and where I met his. It's where we've spent countless hours watching college football and major league baseball games. It's where we've discussed life's joys and hardships until the wee hours of the morning. People will often show up uninvited and unannounced, mainly because the atmosphere is truly so special. However, my brother has one rule: *"If my garage door is open, it's open. If my garage door is closed, it's closed."* He has full control of that door—and yes, he loves us, but this unbendable boundary is healthy for everyone.

We love it when God opens doors of opportunity in our lives. We enter with excitement and anticipation, ready to experience an overflow of blessings. However, in our entitlement, sometimes we interpret a closed door as rejection from something we deserved. We deserved that promotion, but someone else got it. We deserved that new house, but our application was denied. We deserved that fairy-tale relationship, but it ended in heartache.

Satan, being the liar he is, likes to use these situations to twist our thinking, sour our attitude, and crush our confidence. However, here's the truth: a closed door is not due to God's inaction, it's due to His protection in action.

If you're struggling with confidence today, if you painfully face-planted into a door you expected to seamlessly walk through, let me ask you this:

Do you believe God is all-knowing?

Do you believe He knows what's best for you?

Do you believe He wants you to live a healthy, purpose-driven life?

His all-knowing power is there to provide for you *and* to protect you. If that's not love, I don't know what is!

> God, I trust You. May not my will
> but Yours be done. Amen.

# Do It with All Your Heart

*Whatever you do, work heartily, as for the L*ORD *and not for men.*
**COLOSSIANS 3:23 ESV**

In the process of writing this devotional, I started falling into a slump. The deadline was fast approaching, yet I found myself acting like an actual sloth. I was scrolling more than I should, sleeping later than I should, and using every procrastination excuse known to man (including *"I can't write yet, I have to do my Wordle first!"*) Yes, Wordle is a game, and yes, doing that became more important than writing devotions about Jesus.

Eventually, my "I'll do it later" mindset started to affect my confidence. I became anxious that I'd miss the deadline and fearful that I'd run out of things to write. Then I wondered if I was even cut out for this in the first place.

Finally, I'd had enough of my own nonsense. I stood up, threw my shoulders back, and said, "Girl, grow up! Drink some water, shave your hairy sloth legs, and get back to work!" I then a found piece of paper and wrote this note:

"Hannah, whatever work you do, <u>do it with all your heart</u>. <u>Do it for the Lord</u> and not for men. FOCUS!"

Looking at that note on my desk every morning caused

me to hyper-focus on what mattered: writing with all of my heart and doing it for the Lord. And it helped me. A lot.

We often lose confidence in our abilities or in the things we are tasked to do *simply because we aren't doing them wholeheartedly.* We start slipping—becoming careless with our time, lazy in our ethic, and irresponsible with our excuses.

It's not that you're incapable of accomplishing your goal. Not at all, girlfriend! The Bible says you can do all things through Christ, so that's not the issue. The issue lies with *simply losing sight of that goal* and forgetting *Who you're doing it for*. Whether the goal is to get a better job or organize that disaster of a closet, the formula remains the same: Do it *wholeheartedly*, and *do it for the Lord*.

Write down today's verse. Revamp your focus. Do it with all your heart, nothing less!

> God, thank You for today's devotion!
> I commit to leaving procrastination
> behind and working at this with
> my whole heart. Amen.

# Conviction vs. Condemnation

*For God is working in you,*
*giving you the desire and the power*
*to do what pleases Him.*

**PHILIPPIANS 2:13 NLT**

"Welp, you've done it again!" we say to ourselves, with a palm slap to the forehead. We've lost our temper with our kids, we've fallen back into the same old sins, and we feel like absolute skunk poo-poo because of it. Just like Eeyore from *Winnie-the-Pooh*, we wallow in our misfortunes, assuming we will never measure up to the person God wants us to be because we are total *losers*.

Of course we're not losers—but failure has a funny way of stripping our confidence and replacing it with humiliation and guilt. Don't you agree?

Yes, we are human. We are imperfect beings, we fall into temptation, and we cave to our earthly impulses. Some use the "I'm human" excuse to pacify mistakes and avoid accountability. But most people do the opposite, allowing the enemy to inflict blunt-force trauma on their minds with condemnation, depression, and self-loathing. However, let's clear up one thing: there is a huge difference between condemnation and conviction. The enemy condemns, but the Holy Spirit convicts. And friend, conviction is such a good thing! It's the Holy Spirit's gentle way of leading us to a change of heart and His way of lovingly refining our character. Conviction means one thing: that we are passionately adored. It's proof that God is taking the wheel like we've asked Him to. He redirects our paths and saves us from self-inflicted wrecks, because that's what a good Parent does!

God is also full of kindness—when we take responsibility for our actions and sincerely acknowledge our mistakes, God removes our wrongdoings as if they were lost in the depths of the ocean. Now, this doesn't forsake consequences—but it does prove God gives us a clean slate, extends overwhelming forgiveness, and gives us an opportunity to move forward with a newfound desire to please Him.

Research shows that the human brain isn't wired for perfection. Instead, it is wired to adapt! Chasing after perfection isn't the goal, chasing after Jesus is—and when we adapt ourselves to become more like Him, it brews a confidence that changes everything.

> God, I'm grateful for Your conviction.
> I welcome it, because I want my
> character to be more like You. Amen.

# Expecting the Worst

*Be anxious for nothing,
but in everything by prayer
and supplication, with thanksgiving,
let your requests be made known to God;
and the peace of God, which surpasses
all understanding, will guard your hearts
and minds through Christ Jesus.*

PHILIPPIANS 4:6-7 NKJV

You've got your extroverts, you've got your introverts, and then you've got the people in between *(awkwardly raises hand)*. Ambiverts, as they call us, can be social butterflies when necessary, but it's the lead-up to those gatherings that are more draining than the gathering itself. Our minds start to race: *What if it's boring, overstimulating, or awkward?* Or, *What if I accidentally say something super weird?* Or, *Ugh, exerting energy with small talk? Please, God, take this cup from me.* Anyone who is even the slightest bit introverted knows what I'm talking about here!

Whether you're introverted, extroverted, or a little bit of both, all of us can relate to allowing our minds to race, mulling over things that haven't even happened yet. Hypothetical situations play like a movie in our heads, filling us with dread, fear, and insecurity. Interestingly, a study from Cornell University just came out about this very thing. They found that 85 percent of things people worry about never happen, and of the 15 percent that do, 79 percent of people realized the challenge was much easier, and more seamless, than anticipated. In fact, they walked away with greater confidence and learned valuable lessons!

This study was fascinating because it drew me back to the importance of taking our thoughts captive. God is not the author of worry, fear, or failure, and He didn't create us to live that way either! More than likely, our worst assumptions won't happen at all. And even if they do, the Lord will always meet us in the midst of them.

If worry takes over and causes your confidence to shake, remember what it says in Philippians—be anxious for nothing, pray with thanksgiving and gratitude, and make your every request known to the Lord. He will shower you with peace that surpasses all understanding and bring you a confidence that changes everything!

*God, I don't want to always expect the worst. Help me to shine bright in this topsy-turvy life with confidence, knowing that no matter what I face, You will be right there with me. Thank You for making me safe with You. Amen.*

# A Hugged Pot

*Yet You, Lord, are our Father.
We are the clay, You are the potter;
we are all the work of Your hand.*

**ISAIAH 64:8 NIV**

Have you ever heard of a "hugged pot?" Sounds strange, I know. At first glance I assumed the term had to do with drugs *(bless my heart)*. But one day, I came across a "hugged pot" video on Instagram. It's definitely not drugs, guys. Definitely not.

In this reel, two friends with splattered aprons and clay-caked hands were taking a pottery class. After molding together a large pot, with the clay still slightly wet, the friends did something interesting. They sat on either side of the pot, extended their arms, and sandwiched the pot in between a big hug. Once they released their embrace, the pot morphed into a uniquely shaped, cool-looking vase. This adorable experience resulted in a hugged pot that was altogether functional, imperfect yet meaningfully special.

Interestingly enough, Scripture describes a similar pottery experience between us and God. Isaiah 64 says we are the clay, and God is our Potter. I envision this process just like that sweet hugged-pot video: our precious heavenly Father, sitting on a stool with clay-caked hands, forming us with an overwhelming amount of joy and incredible intentionality. He then finishes us off with a loving embrace, a supernatural stamp that causes us to look different and set apart from the rest.

Not only did God form us uniquely in our mother's womb, He continues to mold our characters and hearts today. It's easy for us to get discouraged with imperfections, frustrated with flaws, or annoyed with quirks. But the Lord sees us as a hugged pot—made with love, unique yet purposeful, and continuously sandwiched between the arms of His embrace.

We weren't made to be cookie-cutter perfect. We were made to live out a unique purpose. This goes for every beautiful thing God created: The moon, which is full of craters. The sea, which is salty and dark in the depths. The sky, which is often clouded and gray. Everything God created, even in all its quirks, is not just wondrous and beautiful—it's purposefully special. Yes, including you!

> God, knowing You intentionally formed me, and are still molding me uniquely today, fills me with a newfound confidence that I can't explain. I love You. Thank You for choosing me. Amen.

# A Black Cloud

*Though an army encamp against me,*
*my heart shall not fear;*
*though war arise against me,*
*yet I will be confident.*

PSALM 27:3 ESV

Let's face it—life is tough. Circumstances happen that are so heavy, so intense, so debilitating. During times like this, bee-bopping around with confidence and a million-dollar smile seems impossible and unrealistically annoying. And when people sweep in with that "keep your head up" or "just think positive" nonsense, forget it.

I know the weight of trauma all too well—abuse, betrayal, abandonment, loss. And yes, church hurt too. I fell victim to a deviant youth pastor, a man who groomed me and stole my innocence as a teenage girl, then sued me for speaking out about it years later. I understand, friend, how the unfairness of life can be absolutely crushing.

This might be eyebrow-raising to say, but hear me out. Bad things in life will inevitably happen. But because *we are mortal and flawed beings, we are completely incapable of walking in confidence again without outside help*. Yes, unfortunately, confidence is not man-made. This is why we have to be careful of messages about "self-love" and "I'm enough-ness." We are not designed to heal ourselves.

We are designed to be totally, completely, and helplessly dependent on a *Healer*.

This is why our God is so good. He sent His Son to bear the burden of our sin, shame, pain, and sorrows on the cross. He left us His Spirit—the Holy Spirit—a Comforter, to walk us through the worst of the worst during this temporary time on earth. He also gave us His Word—Scriptures that will renew our minds, restore our hearts, and refresh our souls.

Yes, black clouds can steal our confidence and joy. But staying in the valley is not where God wants us to remain. We must be intentional—intentional in prayer, intentional with Bible reading, intentional with Christian counseling, intentional in surrounding ourselves with godly people. Being intentional allows us to embrace the supernatural help we so desperately need, and reminds us that no matter what, *all things* will work together for good!

> God, You are my Healer. You are where my help comes from. I choose to be intentional with You today, for it is You alone who brings me confidence. Amen.

# The Snowball Effect of Joy

*Joyful are people of integrity,
who follow the instructions of the Lord.
Joyful are those who obey His laws and search for
Him with all their hearts. They do not compromise
with evil, and they walk only in His paths.*

PSALM 119:1-4 NLT

My first devotional book, *Goodness Gracious: 90 Unfiltered Devotions for this Sometimes-Too-Serious Life,* is centered around the topic of joy *(emphasis on the word* unfiltered, *guys. I use wild phrases like "bologna snot" and share stories that would make you spit coffee out of your nose).* In all seriousness though, the more I learned about the true meaning of joy during that writing process, the more I realized how life-changing joy truly is. It has a snowball effect: joy causes healing; healing produces strength; strength leads to smiles; smiles overflow with laughter; laughter draws in new people; new people turn into meaningful relationships; and meaningful relationships open up greater doors of opportunity to shine the light of Jesus.

People often believe *if they only* had more money, *if they only* had a prettier face, *if they only* had more talents, it would be easier to walk in confidence. But after recognizing the snowball effect of joy, it appears to be the one thing that effortlessly leads to confidence. Psalm 119 offers another valuable perspective on joy—a "secret sauce" that allows people to keep this snowball effect going. Joyful people constantly possess three things:

1. *Integrity*. Joyful people operate with good character and gratitude in all circumstances!
2. *Obedience*. Joyful people obey the laws of God and wholeheartedly search for Him on a daily basis!
3. *Godliness*. Joyful people don't compromise by entertaining evil thoughts or actions. They know this can damage their life, relationships, and legacy. Instead, they adopt the Lord's thoughts and actions!

All three of these—integrity, obedience, and godliness—are centered in Christ. And as we know, when Christ is the center of our lives, it leads to a confidence that changes everything!

Joy is the kind of happiness that doesn't depend on what happens. Life's problems will always be a thing. But it's the snowball effect of joy that can effortlessly lead us to confidence and a life full of light!

> God, I see the value joy can bring to my life. Let joy overflow within me, so I can walk in confidence. Amen.

# Observe, Regulate, Adjust

*Let us examine and probe our ways,
and let us return to the L*ORD.
**LAMENTATIONS 3:40 NASB1995**

It happens when we walk into our boss's office. It creeps up when we see popular Instagram influencers. It arises when we run into that girl from high school or when we attend highfalutin events.

"It" refers to feelings that brew insecurity—fear, excitement, awe, jealousy, inspiration, resentment, anticipation—all mixed together like ingredients in a tuna salad. In these situations, our nervous systems become unstable, which is about as fun as riding a rickety roller coaster from 1955!

It's impossible to stay bubble-wrapped in a comfortable cave filled with Care Bears, guys. The real world is wild, unpredictable, and stressful. So, *how can we live confidently as good examples of Jesus, without allowing insecurity to control how we live?*

Emotions are from the Lord. God feels things, just like we do. However, He allows us to feel things not so we can be ruled by them but as a reminder to pray and release control. Instead of laying our feelings down at His feet, we sometimes place them on a makeshift throne—idolizing them rather than surrendering them.

Dr. Caroline Leaf, a world-renowned pathologist and neuroscientist, lists three helpful tips when it comes to battling insecurity:

1. *Observe.* Take a step back and ask yourself, *Why am I feeling insecure? What messages am I sending myself? How is this affecting how I function?*
2. *Regulate.* When we recognize our feelings, we can better regulate ourselves with greater wisdom and grace.
3. *Adjust.* Regulating leads to making adjustments in our thoughts and actions. When we adjust, we can prevent little things from throwing us off-kilter and disrupting our confidence.

The next time big feelings emerge, remember to surrender them to the Lord—then observe, regulate, and adjust. God is for you, never against you. He can help you confidently embrace your identity in Christ, even on the hard days!

**God, I surrender every insecurity to You. Help me to walk confidently in You. Amen.**

# Answered and Unanswered

*Do not be like them,
for your Father knows what
you need before you ask Him.*

MATTHEW 6:8 NIV

There is nothing more confidence-boosting than when God answers our prayers. We can't help ourselves: shamelessly shouting His praises like a middle-aged football dad, enthusiastically spreading His goodness like a kid with a jar of Nutella. We asked for something, He pulled through, and we're happy campers! Knowing He truly hears us when we speak fills our hearts with excitement, relief, and gratitude.

Yet, we don't feel that same confidence when God seemingly sends our call to voicemail. We start to wonder, *God, do You hear me at all? Are You even good? Why are You not intervening in the way You should?*

It's easy to trust God when His answer is "yes." But when His answer is "no," or if there is silence, our faith starts to shake. During this time of uncertainty is when the enemy loves to strike: "See? God doesn't hear you. He doesn't love you. Quit praying, it doesn't work anyway!"

However, Scripture tells us that prayer is something

we should do without ceasing. God doesn't just welcome our prayers of gratitude and praise, He welcomes our prayers of confusion and anguish. We see King David do this throughout the book of Psalms—in one breath he praised God by dancing in the streets, in the next breath he cried out to God in despair while hiding in a cave.

Matthew 6 tells us that our Father knows what we need even before we ask Him. As much of a bummer as it feels to have a prayer go unanswered, God is always up to something. He is either protecting us, teaching us, or guiding us in a way that aligns with His perfect will. How easily we forget Whom we're talking to: the God of the universe, the God who holds the future, the God who loves us so much He sent His only Son!

Hold tight in prayer today, no matter how He answers. Your precious heavenly Father knows exactly what you need. Be confident today knowing that He not only hears you, but He is holding your broken heart in the palm of His hand!

*God, I will not stop praying. I trust You hear me, and I trust Your answers no matter what. Amen.*

# The Daily Seven

*Make the most of every opportunity
in these evil days.*
EPHESIANS 5:16 NLT

In a world of social media scrolling, Netflix binging, and increased isolation, it's no wonder we struggle with confidence! Messages of inferiority swirl around our minds like a flushing toilet bowl, and the enemy loves it. In fact, that good-for-nothin' loser knows if he can keep us in the bondage of insecurity, it will stunt our effectiveness for the kingdom of God!

Sometimes we overcomplicate what it takes to walk in confidence. Maybe it's just a simple tweak that can dramatically improve our quality of life! Which of the following "Daily Seven" can you implement?

1. *Time with God.* Reading God's Word, praying, and listening to worship music creates peace, intimacy, and trust. It's the best way to renew one's mind!
2. *Daily goals.* Create a to-do list of things to accomplish. Achieving even something small is a confidence booster, especially when doing it for the Lord!
3. *Exercise.* A thirty-minute workout is all we need! Not only are we proud of ourselves afterward, we feel better and think clearer throughout the day.

4. *Go outside.* Sunlight and fresh air are gifts from God, and essential for our health. Walking barefoot on the earth is also extremely beneficial!
5. *Servanthood.* Pour into the lives of others. We must extend our God-given gifts without expecting anything in return. Volunteering our time and thinking of others rather than ourselves is exactly what Jesus calls us to do!
6. *Creative Expression.* Painting, journaling, music, crafting. Whatever it may be, spending time each day to foster creativity promotes confidence, beauty, and healing.
7. *Fellowship.* Spend time with godly friends to restore your soul. Join a small group, grab coffee with a friend, invite someone over for dinner. We are built for community—to pour out into others, and to be poured into ourselves!

Confidence comes when we manage our time, gifts, and relationships wisely. Sometimes all it takes is going back to the basics! Let's grow in our "Daily Seven," and live with intention and purpose!

> God, this "Daily Seven" list is so simple and helpful. I am excited to implement these good habits and grow with confidence in You! Amen.

Confidence comes when we manage our time, gifts, and relationships wisely.

# Operate in Your Gifts

*For the gifts and the calling of God are irrevocable.*
**ROMANS 11:29 ESV**

Early on, we could tell our daughter was *totally extra*. She would hilariously reenact her favorite TV shows with bubbly enthusiasm. She would sing or dance for anyone, at any time, without a stitch of shyness. Her performance-driven personality exuded so much sass, spunk, and charisma that it didn't surprise us one bit when she fell in love with the arts. For most people, standing on a stage or looking into a camera is the most frightening place on the planet. But for her, it's where she comes alive.

Our son, on the other hand, has a totally different set of gifts. He can look at a math problem and solve it without skipping a beat. He can build the coolest sculptures using Legos, sticks, and dead bugs. He quickly masters athletic skills in ways that are quite impressive. And let me just tell you, if there was ever a job opening for a professional dinosaur roar-er, he would absolutely crush it.

While the Lord was knitting you in your mother's womb, He was also weaving in special intricacies—talents, traits, and gifts that set you apart from everyone else. This was purposeful! Your gifting isn't just a fun little flair to who you are—it is a large part of your calling!

Sometimes we get tricked into believing that our gifts aren't *that* cool, or that people would find them *annoying*, or that they're *not important enough* to make a difference. Maybe we even think that because our gifts can't necessarily provide for us financially, they're not worth using. However, that is not the point of a gift. A gift is given by God for one reason—to use it, and to use it for His glory. When we do, it not only brings others great joy, it brings us great joy too!

If we want to walk in confidence, we *must* operate in our gifts. Ask the Lord today to show you ways to utilize the talents within you to bless those around you. It doesn't matter what this gift looks like—or whether it's public or behind the scenes. Every gift is a valuable, necessary, precious treasure that will allow you to shine bright in this topsy-turvy life!

> God, show me how to
> use my gifts in new ways.
> I desire to give You glory. Amen.

# Beware of Sharks

*Whoever isolates himself
seeks his own desire;
he breaks out against
all sound judgment.*

PROVERBS 18:1 ESV

Sharks have always freaked me out. My cousins *made me* watch *Jaws* when I was young because they thought my expressions were *"so funny,"* those little twerps. However, this fear of sharks drove me to learn more about them. Despite what the movie protrays, sharks don't usually attack when there are tons of people around. They usually wait to take a curious bite when someone is by themselves.

We've touched on the dangers of isolation, but let's expand on this a little more. We live in a connection-deprived culture—we don't *need* to meet up with people, because the internet has become its own social circle. However, this has made our generation more anxious, depressed, and lonely than ever before. The enemy, like a shark, loves to strike when we're alone. He warps our thoughts, twists our perceptions, and skews our reality.

I'll take this one step further. Online church has become incredibly popular. It's more convenient to sit at home in our jammies than to get dressed and sit in a pew *(also, avoiding that awkward "greet your neighbor" scenario sounds very appealing)*. However, here's the issue—if we're struggling, nobody can hug us through a computer screen. If we're hurting, no one can lay hands on us to pray. While online church has its place, Jesus set a different example. The body of Christ is designed for experiencing the move of God together, in person.

What does this have to do with confidence? Well, for one, isolation makes us insecure, and it throws confidence out the window. It also makes life much harder than if we had friends to step in when things get heavy. I love the analogy of a workhorse: one horse can pull up to 8,000 pounds. But when he has another horse beside him, they don't pull 16,000 pounds—together, they can pull up to 24,000 pounds! As the saying goes, "the math ain't mathing"—but it doesn't have to, because the same goes for us as believers. We can walk with greater confidence knowing we have people around us, in person, to help carry the load.

> God, I know the value of being there for people, and not just behind a screen. Help me to get excited about in-person fellowship and connection. Amen.

# Oh Be Careful, Little Eyes

*The eye is the lamp of the body.*
*If your eyes are healthy,*
*your whole body will be full of light.*
*But if your eyes are unhealthy,*
*your whole body will be full of darkness.*

MATTHEW 6:22-23 NIV

While my greatest childhood fear was being eaten alive by sharks, my youngest sister, Payton, also had a childhood fear—that of being kidnapped. Payton never wanted to sleep alone. Every night, she would eventually crawl in bed with my parents or with me. I loved it when I was chosen as her "nightly protector"—mainly because she was darling, an adorable, life-sized Cabbage Patch Kid. But I knew to beware, for underneath all that cuteness was the rage of a rabid raccoon. If I dared to console Payton's fears with a hug, she would scream "Stooooop-uh!", sock me straight in the nose, and fall fast asleep with zero remorse. Just the sweetest little bundle of joy!

We never knew why my sister was so afraid of being kidnapped, until she revealed the truth—she had watched a news segment about Elizabeth Smart. Seeing this scary kidnapping story on TV developed into one of her greatest fears, just like watching *Jaws* birthed my fear of sharks.

Shakespeare referred to the eyes as the windows to the soul, and he was absolutely right. The things we see with our eyes *matters*—the movies we watch, the Netflix shows we binge, the news we consume. Whether we want to believe it or not, the harmful things we see can negatively affect us on an emotional and spiritual level, causing us to walk in fear instead of walking in confidence. The enemy uses media to have a heyday with our minds, causing us to think irrational thoughts and react in irrational ways.

Let's be honest with ourselves:

Do we *have* to see horror films? No.

Do we *need* to keep up with every news story 24/7? No.

Should we consciously fill our eyes with beautiful things, godly things, allowing the Lord to fill us with a confidence that changes everything? Yes!

So let's guard the gates of our eyes. May we no longer allow the things we watch to lead us down a road of fear!

> God, I no longer want fear to steal my confidence. Help me to resist temptation with what my eyes behold. Amen.

# Have Fun!

*Also that everyone should
eat and drink and take pleasure
in all his toil—this is God's gift to man.*
**ECCLESIASTES 3:13 ESV**

Have you ever heard of the term "fun-sucker"? It's basically directed to anyone or anything that sucks the fun out of life. For me, those are things like standing in line at the DMV, doing my taxes, or Karens. *(Kidding! Again, I have an Aunt Karen. She's nice.)* In any case, life is no fun if things aren't—well—fun!

I played basketball growing up, and there was one school we dreaded competing against. They were scrappy, they were mean, they'd viciously mock us and throw cheap shots when the referee wasn't looking. Even though my teammates and I loved the sport, playing against this team wasn't fun. That is, until one day, our coach gave us a pep talk that changed our attitude. She reminded us that we were not only great players, we were set apart because of Christ within us. Therefore, we had no reason to allow anything *(or anyone)* to steal our joy while playing the game we loved! Our perspective shifted from fear to fun, and the scoreboard reflected it. Little did we know, intentionally choosing to have fun gave us a confidence that changed everything!

We are called to let our light shine among all men. But in order to allow that light to shine, we need to exhibit an attitude of joy! Obviously, joy comes when we're having fun. Yet, the fact is, life isn't always fun—it's hard, it's intimidating, and it's even scary sometimes.

However, the Bible is clear—the joy of the Lord gives us strength to face things we dread. What if we shifted our perspective during the fun-sucking times and found a way to add in some enjoyment? Maybe it's listening to upbeat music while in line at the DMV. Maybe it's doing our taxes poolside with a charcuterie board. Or maybe it's blessing every Karen with a *(genuine)* smile and a *(not sarcastically spoken)* kind word!

I encourage you to read the book of Ecclesiastes. King Solomon speaks lots of wisdom on the importance of enjoying life and not taking things too seriously! Fun brings joy, and joy brings confidence!

> God, I rejoice in this new day to live for You! May the fun I have today cause me to walk in confidence. Amen.

# Stimulate Wholesome Thinking

*Finally, brothers and sisters,
whatever is true, whatever is noble,
whatever is right, whatever is pure,
whatever is lovely, whatever is admirable—
if anything is excellent or praiseworthy—
think about such things.*
PHILIPPIANS 4:8 NIV

When I look back on some of the worst times of my life, I recall how I felt—depressed, hopeless, insecure, wounded, and broken. I felt a lot like Ron Burgundy when he lost his job in the movie *Anchorman*, disheveled and stuck in a glass case of emotion *(if you've seen the movie, you know how funny this is)*.

But praise the Lord for godly friends and godly counsel! Surrounding myself with believers who not only listened but imparted great wisdom helped me heal much more effectively. One piece of consistent advice I received was this:

*"If a thought is plaguing your mind, robbing your peace or stealing your sleep, you must take that thought captive!"*

But whoa, how do we do that? It's not like we can just slap some handcuffs on our brains. That's unrealistic and goofy. However, what we can do is this: *stimulate wholesome thinking.*

In the book of Second Peter, Peter says his reason for writing to the persecuted church was to "stimulate wholesome thinking" in their minds. He reminded Christians of many prophetic promises, the imminence of the Lord's return, and the value of living blamelessly for Christ. If we think our own life is hard, can we *only imagine* how it was to face death *just for being a Christian*? Even Peter knew that if those believers could actively stimulate wholesome thinking, they could endure the worst.

Our thoughts can either boost our confidence or tear it down. One way of thinking is God's way, the other way of thinking is the enemy's. If our thoughts are robbing our peace or stealing our sleep, we must ask ourselves: Are these thoughts from the Lord? Is this how He thinks of me? Is this the way He wants me to think?

This is why I love Philippians 4:8 so much. It gives us a blueprint on what to think when our thinking stinks. Shifting our thoughts—and being surrounded with godly people—can stimulate a confidence that changes everything!

God, I need to take my thoughts captive. Thank You for reminding me to seek wisdom from godly influences and to actively pursue wholesome thinking. Amen.

# Unusual Wisdom

*God also gave Joseph unusual wisdom, so that Pharoah appointed him governor over all of Egypt and put him in charge of the palace.*
ACTS 7:10 NLT

There's a popular quote going around that I absolutely love. It says this:

*"I'm not embarrassed by anything I've gone through. What may be 'tea' for you, is a testimony for me!"*

Shame loves to attach itself to the mistakes we've made or the pain we've endured. Whether we've experienced divorce, failed in business, or driven away with the gas pump still attached *(that one's both embarrassing and slightly funny)*—we all have something that haunts us to this day. Shame shatters our confidence, but one hopeful truth remains: great disappointment often leads to great wisdom!

The dictionary defines *wisdom* as "the quality of having experience, knowledge, and good judgment." Yes, we gain wisdom from our successes, but wisdom is mainly gained through our struggles. Let's take Joseph for example: He was wildly favored and over-the-top successful. However, he went through unimaginable betrayal and misrepresentation to get there. Because of this, God gave him unusual wisdom— and unusual wisdom comes from going through unusual circumstances.

It wasn't just Joseph who gained unusual wisdom through his circumstances. Many others in the Bible did too:

**David had wisdom** *because he learned from the consequences of his disobedience and sin.*

**Peter had wisdom** *because he remembered how shameful it felt after denying Jesus.*

**Mary Magdalene had wisdom** *because she experienced Christ's grace despite her past.*

The Word also says that every good and perfect gift comes from above. If we're desperately wanting wisdom, we can simply ask for it! Receiving unusual wisdom comes by pursuing the One who created it. Others in the Bible did just that:

**Gideon had wisdom** in the military *because he requested that God provide him with a strategy.*

**Esther had wisdom** to save her people *because she fasted and prayed for God to help her.*

**Solomon had wisdom** to build wealth and success *because he asked God for only one gift—the gift of wisdom.*

Yes, you have walked through many unusual circumstances. However, God will use the darkest parts of your testimony to forge unusual wisdom within you! That, my friend, restores a confidence that changes everything!

*God, You are the Author of all wisdom. I choose to seek You today, because following You is where I grow the most. Amen.*

# Be a Prepper

*Therefore you also must be ready, for the Son of Man is coming at an hour you do not expect.*

MATTHEW 24:44 ESV

Do you know anyone who is a doomsday prepper? They prepare for events like a market crash, a grid shutdown, or a zombie apocalypse. They hoard all kinds of things, from dried beans to antibiotics. You might even find them practicing random skills like archery or jiu-jitsu. I, for one, have never been a prepper. But let me just tell you, when 2020 hit, I sure did miss having enough toilet paper, if you know what I mean!

When we are unprepared, our confidence takes a hit. This goes for anything from school tests, to work presentations, to sports competitions, to unforeseen curveballs in life. When we realize we're not ready for the reality of what's in front of us, we feel completely vulnerable and insecure.

The Bible talks a bunch about being prepared—however, God isn't necessarily telling us to stock up on water bottles *(even though that's always a good idea)*. Instead, He consistently reminds us to prepare our hearts for the return of Jesus. Just like we don't know when we will take our last breath, we don't know when He's coming back. Regardless of if we see Jesus descending from the clouds or if we see Him on Judgment Day, we must start prepping ourselves now!

Confidence in our abilities is dependent on our level of preparation, and with preparation comes practice! Practice can be grueling, painful, refining, and redundant—however, it is necessary for us to be successful. The same goes for preparing for eternity—we must ready our hearts and cultivate our walk with Christ. We prepare by reflecting on our choices, renewing our mindset, and letting go of our own plans to embrace His.

I guess being a prepper isn't that weird, after all! In fact, it brings a confidence that changes everything! Whatever you're preparing for today, do it with excellence. Prepare your mind, prepare your body, and prepare your heart for what's to come. Let's be good preppers for both our everyday responsibilities and for the eternity that lies before us!

> God, I don't want to get caught in a state of unreadiness with anything in my life. I choose to prepare myself today, and most importantly, to prepare my heart. Amen.

# Blur the Distractions

*Let your eyes look directly forward,
and your gaze be straight before you.*
PROVERBS 4:25 ESV

When I was a freshman in high school, I picked up pole vaulting. The sport was so cool to me, especially how a person could jump that high with only speed and a stick. But here's the kicker—I am terrified of heights! Why I chose a sport that is the equivalent of falling from a two-story building is beyond me. Even though I was good, sometimes fear would grip me so greatly that it would leave me with a severe case of bubble gut.

My coach was a wise man. He knew how to snap me out of every mental funk. On the morning of the regional finals, he brought me to the stadium before dawn. There wasn't a soul in sight—just us, the track, and silence. He told me to stare at the high bar, blur out everything else around me, and visualize myself clearing it with ease. With no distractions, this was easy. But then he said, "This afternoon, when the stadium is filled and the nerves are high, I want you to do the same thing: stare at the high bar, blur out everything else around you, and visualize yourself clearing it with ease." It worked, and I won the bronze medal.

Sometimes in order to walk in confidence, we have to visualize our goal with tunnel vision. It's easy to compare ourselves to others or be fearful of the obstacles. However, success only happens when we paint a successful picture in our minds. This goes for everyday activities too! Instead of being overwhelmed by the mess in our kitchen, closet, or backyard, we must visualize it looking clean, organized, and pristine. Mentally picturing the best possible outcome will help us to achieve the best possible outcome!

There is such power in our thoughts. Our mind can lead us down a road of failure, or it can lead us up the path toward victory. When we renew our minds with God's Word and blur out the distractions that hold us back, it brings a confidence that changes everything!

*God, help me to have tunnel vision today. I choose to focus on the goal, blur out all the distractions, and visualize victory. Thank You for walking with me, hand in hand. Amen.*

# I'm Not Cut Out for This!

*Then the LORD asked Moses, "Who makes a person's mouth? Who decides whether people speak or do not speak, hear or do not hear, see or do not see? Is it not I, the LORD?"*

**EXODUS 4:11 NLT**

I'm just not cut out for this!" How many times have we said that when things got hard? If it's out of our element or beyond our skill set, we immediately disqualify ourselves. I once felt this way when someone asked me to translate for a guy who spoke Spanish. My *español* is decent, but this spontaneous request made my brain freeze. I couldn't make out a word this guy said *(though I'm pretty sure he cursed a little).*

Moses also felt this way when God called him to lead the Israelites out of Egypt. This would mean he'd have to speak to Pharoah, and that, my friends, was a big, big problem. Not only was Moses wanted for killing a dude, he also had a speech impediment. Surely, God had lost His marbles this time—choosing a stuttering felon to approach the leader of Egypt? Weird move.

However, God never coddled Moses' insecurities. Instead, He reminded Moses of Who He was, and redirected

Moses' attention from inward to upward. The only reason Moses was successful was because God is the definition of success. Obeying God was all Moses needed to walk in confidence and to walk in victory.

When God gives us an assignment, He sets us up for success. God isn't going to coddle our insecurities—because quite frankly, our insecurities are diddly-squat compared to His almighty power. We can do all kinds of big, scary, intimidating things when we quit focusing on ourselves and start focusing on the Lord.

Yet, even in our humanness, God will always show up with patience and grace. If insecurity causes your knees to shake or your brain to freeze, don't worry—God will equip you. Your obedience, not your qualifications, is all He needs.

Remember this:

God gave you those children.

God gave you that job.

God gave you those gifts.

If He believes you are the perfect fit for that assignment, *who are you to say you're not?*

God is with you, always. That brings a confidence that changes everything!

> God, with You,
> I'm cut out for anything.
> I choose to obey and answer
> every call. Amen.

# The Heat of Pressure

*Blessed is the one who perseveres under trial because, having stood the test, that person will receive the crown of life that the Lord has promised to those who love Him.*

**JAMES 1:12 NIV**

As much as I love my babies, giving birth to them was a trip. Those contractions were out-of-this-world bananas—and don't even get me started on that ring of fire! Of course, the moment my babies were placed on my chest, I forgot every ounce of agony it took to get them there. Leaning into the pressure, the heat, and the pain led to such a precious reward. *(Also, if childbirth is part of your future, fear not! Just know that, yes, it's perfectly normal to grunt and honk like a four-thousand-pound walrus. It's fine, it's fine, it's all fine.)*

The pressures of life are everywhere. Whether it's a verbal confrontation, a hard-fought championship, or a stressful job—pressure happens. And every time we face it, we're forced to make a split-second decision on how to handle it.

Because pressure is uncomfortable, we are often guilty of running from it. The tension, the comparison, and the fear of failure become heavy, causing us to crack and crumble. However, the most confident people in the world choose to lean into the pressure rather than push against it. They know the fire isn't there to burn them, the fire is there to refine them. Confident people embrace the pressure, and they grow through it victoriously.

A diamond, too, experiences an intense amount of heat and pressure, causing carbon atoms to crystallize into a splendid jewel. Because of this extreme process, a diamond develops brilliance, strength, and beauty—all of which heighten its desirability and value.

You, my dearest friend, are also a jewel—more precious than rubies, in fact. And God has crowned you with a special gifting, a unique and mighty assignment.

Is your calling going to be heavy at times? Yes.

Will the pressures of life heat up unexpectedly? You bet.

But can you do all things through Christ who gives you strength? Absolutely!

> God, I know that pressure isn't always a bad thing. Lead me through the fire, and instill within me a confidence that changes everything. Amen.

God has crowned you with a special gifting, a unique and mighty assignment.

# Rest Is Best

*"Come to me,
all of you who are weary
and carry heavy burdens,
and I will give you rest*

MATTHEW 11:28 NLT

If running around like a chicken with your head cut off is normal for you, come sit by me. Not only because I can relate but because we need to sit down anyway. Our ankles are starting to swell and our heart rate is sounding like a woodpecker. Also, when's the last time we had any water? Let's take a break together. Today's devotion will help too.

In our quest for confidence, we sometimes misconstrue success with "no days off." We believe being a "boss babe" means staying on call 24/7. We believe being a good parent means packing our schedules to the brim. We believe being prosperous means putting in extra work that no one else will.

While diligence and excellence are valuable and important, this "grind it out" culture we live in today is actually *(gasp)* quite toxic! In fact, it goes against God's design for us from the beginning of time.

When God rested on the seventh day of creation, He did this as an example for how we should live. He refers to this day as the Sabbath, which is defined as an abstinence from work. When we overlook this and burn the candle at both ends, we become burned out, fatigued, and discouraged. Lack of rest causes us to perform half-heartedly rather than wholeheartedly, and scientifically, it messes with our mind and weakens our body.

The Sabbath also has another meaning. The book of Leviticus refers to the Sabbath as a day of God-centered observation and holy assembly. Not only is it a day for worshipping God, it is a day for assembling in the house of God! Gathering with other believers and hearing God's Word refreshes the mind and restores the soul. Therefore, attending a weekly service isn't work, it's rest! Instead of skipping church because we are tired, we must go to church *because we are tired*!

If we want to walk in confidence, we must unplug from work and plug into our Savior. He is the only one who can recharge our souls like never before!

Thanks for sitting down with me on this one. You can get up now.

> God, I vow to honor the Sabbath.
> I will rest, be still, and know
> that You are God. Amen.

# Live to Give

*Each one must give
as he has decided in his heart,
not reluctantly or under compulsion,
for God loves a cheerful giver.*

II CORINTHIANS 9:7 ESV

Allowance day was exciting as a kid. Sure, the sound of quarters dropping into the piggy bank was satisfying. Sure, splurging on Beanie Babies and clothes at Limited Too was a blast. *(Wow, did that sentence just age me or what?)* However, my favorite part about allowance day was setting aside "giving money." This small portion of coins would sometimes go into the offering plate at church; other times it would go into the tin can of a homeless woman; other times it would go into the pocket of a friend at school. Seeing others happy made *me* happy, and it flooded my heart with confidence.

I have seen firsthand how much better it is to give than to receive—and I'm not just referring to finances. Giving of our time, our resources, our talents, our words—all are equally valuable in the sight of the Lord. No matter what or how we give, doing this with a cheerful heart instills a confidence that changes everything!

The important thing about giving, though, is to do it without expecting anything in return. However, this is a hard concept to grasp in today's culture. Most people expect to be *given to* way more than they *give of themselves*. This "scratch my back and I'll scratch yours" mentality often results in strained relationships and unmet expectations, and a dialogue of self-pity starts to surface:

"Why hasn't she spent that kind of time with *me*?"

"Why didn't they give cool gifts like that to *me*?"

"Why doesn't he offer to serve and help *me*?"

Thoughts like this are destructive—and before you know it, gratitude and selflessness are replaced with entitlement and envy. However, the quickest antidote to this—the easiest way to avoid a life of internal misery and walk in godly confidence—*is to be a giver who requires nothing back*.

Giving brings fulfilment, purpose, and joy. It is a beautiful display of selfless exceptionalism—and when done with the right motive, giving is a spiritual medicine that can contagiously heal both others and yourself. When we give, we live!

God, Your Word says
it is better to give than to receive.
Allow me the chance to be
a cheerful giver today. Amen.

# It's How We Say It

*A soft answer turns away wrath,*
*but a harsh word stirs up anger.*
**PROVERBS 15:1 ESV**

In college, I took an improvisation acting class. One day, the professor told us to act out one phrase in a variety of ways. I can't remember the exact line, but let's use the phrase "You're awesome" for example. I spoke with two differing mannerisms:

1. "You're awesome!" *(open smile, eyebrows raised, high-pitched voice)* as if I'm congratulating my bestie on landing her dream job.
2. "You're awesome. . ." *(frown, eye roll, low-pitched voice)* as if I'm validating my husband for taking out the trash even though I asked him forty-five times.

This assignment proved it's not *what we say* but *how we say it* that matters—both on stage and in life.

Recently, I read a profound story in the book of Luke, and it paralleled the lesson I learned in acting class. In summary, the story goes like this:

*The angel Gabriel told Zechariah he'd have a son.*
*Zechariah replied, "But how can this happen?*
*My wife and I are old."*

*The angel Gabriel chastised Zechariah for his faithless response and made him mute.*
*The angel Gabriel told Mary she'd have a son.*
*Mary replied, "But how can this happen? I am a virgin."*
*The angel Gabriel did not chastise her;*
*instead, he gently explained how it would happen.*

Zechariah and Mary spoke nearly identical verbiage, but they had two very different outcomes. Knowing Mary's character, we can accurately assume her heart was in the right place. However, Zechariah was probably being a little snarky. The Bible says out of the abundance of the heart the mouth speaks. Yes, our words matter, but the heart behind our words matters most.

Maybe we're clueless as to how we come across sometimes—and we continue to struggle in personal and professional relationships. We must be honest with ourselves if our communication isn't working! Do our words come from a place of anger, jealousy, bitterness, or pride? Do our comments reflect an attitude of grumbling, complaining, or negativity?

A contrite spirit will lead to Christlike communication. When our hearts and our words align with Jesus, it leads to favor with both God and man—and that will bring a confidence that changes everything!

> God, I want my heart and words to look and sound more like You. Amen.

# The Bible Is a Mirror

*For if anyone is a hearer
of the word and not a doer,
he is like a man who looks intently
at his natural face in a mirror.
For he looks at himself and goes away
and at once forgets what he was like.
But the one who looks into the perfect law,
the law of liberty, and perseveres,
being no hearer who forgets
but a doer who acts,
he will be blessed in his doing.*
JAMES 1:23-25 ESV

Mulan was one of my favorite Disney characters growing up. This princess wasn't fancy or gentle; she was quirky and a total gangster. Because she was different, it led her down a lonely path of self-discovery that most of us can relate to. We all desire to belong, to know our purpose, to make a difference in this world.

Sure, the movie was great, but the soundtrack was *baller*. Christina Aguilera's rendition of the song "Reflection" quickly became one of the most profound Disney tunes of all time because it speaks to what we see in the mirror.

Many of us tend to overly magnify every imperfection. We see our face and compare it to the faces of others. We see our body and feel disappointment, frustration, or shame.

However, even though man looks at the outward appearance, the Lord looks at the heart. Instead of trying to improve what we see in the mirror, we must focus on improving the reflection of our character! Doing this is simple and straightforward when we use the Bible as a mirror. Peering into the pages of Scripture reflects the deepest parts of our hearts—the parts that God wants to refine and perfect.

A physical mirror cannot truly fix the way we look, but the spiritual mirror of God's Word can fix our hearts. When we allow Him to beautify us on the inside, the light of Jesus shines through us on the outside!

*God, Your Spirit is
the most beautiful part about me.
May I always be
a doer of Your Word. Amen.*

# Betrayal of Confidence

*Argue your case with your neighbor himself,
and do not reveal another's secret,
lest he who hears you bring shame upon you,
and your ill repute have no end.*

**PROVERBS 25:9-10 ESV**

It's easy to wake up on the confident side of the bed when life is peachy. You slip on a fluffy robe, twist your hair up in rollers, and fill up your "Not Today, Satan" coffee mug. As you joyfully bee-bop into the office with a cute "laugh without fear of the future" attitude, you suddenly notice something weird—your coworkers are whispering, snickering, and acting totally sus.

Come to find out, your work bestie Karen told everyone your big secret. The mystery smell in the office yesterday was actually *your tummy*, not the boss's twelve-year-old dog. Goodness gracious, no one would have *ever known* if she hadn't spilled the beans about your reaction to...well, beans. Thanks a lot, Chipotle. And thanks for nothing, Karen *(again, no offense to Karens. I love you, Aunt Karen!)*

Being confident is one thing, but it's another ballgame when someone betrays your confidence. Betrayal *literally* stinks. And while the hypothetical scene above sounds like it belongs in a comedy movie, it doesn't take away from how much it hurts to be let down by someone you trust. Not only does it damage your current relationship, it plants seeds of doubt and cynicism toward future relationships too.

The saddest thing about betrayal is it never comes from an enemy. Jesus knew this all too well—one of His besties pretended like he didn't know Him, and His other bestie turned Him in for a bag of cash. I'm sure Jesus was tempted to do what we want to do—clap back, return fire, or seek revenge—but He didn't.

The only way to truly recover from betrayal is forgiveness. I know, that's hard. However, forgiveness doesn't excuse their behavior, it just prevents their behavior from destroying your heart. Doing this restores your joy, gives you rest, and acts as a humble reminder of how you've also been forgiven. Forgiveness doesn't always equate to reconciliation, but it does hold the power to break every chain.

Life will betray you. But guess what? God never will!

> God, I know walking in forgiveness brings a confidence that changes everything. Heal my heart when my confidence is betrayed. Amen.

# Choices, Choices

*What then shall we say to these things?*
*If God is for us, who can be against us?*
ROMANS 8:31 ESV

I once decided to put wallpaper in my bathroom. We knew a full remodel was impending anyway, so the idea of sassing it up with some fun wallpaper was exciting. I ordered a bunch of swatches, probably twenty-five different styles, and impatiently awaited their arrival. Finally, the day came—I ripped open the package and dumped every swatch onto my living room floor. I thought I'd be able to quickly narrow it down, but that simply wasn't the case. The more options I saw, the more undecided I felt, and the more I toiled over the possibilities, the more I started to question if I wanted wallpaper at all. Even though I almost called it quits, I finally picked a pattern that worked. Now that bathroom is my favorite part of the house!

Despite what you may have been told, walking in confidence is a choice. It's not something you're born with, it's something you learn. In life, we are presented with all kinds of choices, and these choices can be hard, exciting, unpredictable, fun. But each time we are presented with a choice, we also have to decide how we will approach it.

According to Dr. David L. Cook, a famous sports psychologist, our thoughts determine the outcome of every choice or opportunity. In life or in performance, we are presented with six mental thoughts:

1. *I won't.* Hard stop. It's not happening, so I'm not trying.
2. *I can't.* Whether it's true or not, I'm telling myself it's not possible.
3. *I'd like to.* It would be great, but I'm not sure if I want to put in the effort.
4. *I'll try.* I'll put in some effort, but disappointments may ruin the outcome.
5. *I can.* I am capable of this, but let's just hope I stay driven enough.
6. *I will.* No matter what, it's happening.

When we mentally choose the "I will" approach, we embrace the entire journey—the hard stuff *(pressure, practice, perseverance)* and the victory that awaits at the finish line. Confidence is a choice—a choice that says "*I can* and *I will* do all things through Christ who strengthens me!"

> God, give me an "I will" kind of confidence. No more excuses—with You, all things are possible! Amen.

# What Money Can't Buy

*Then Mary took a twelve-ounce jar
of expensive perfume made from the essence of nard,
and she anointed Jesus' feet with it,
wiping His feet with her hair.
The house was filled with the fragrance.*

JOHN 12:3 NLT

And this is why I can't have nice things!" These famous words echoed from my mouth after I spilled an entire bottle of black nail polish onto my white rug. You'd think I was talking to my dogs or my kids, but no. I was yelling at my clumsy little self. *It's me, hi, I'm the problem. It's me.*

It's such a gut punch to watch our money go down the drain. We work so hard to earn what we have, and when our finances are shaky, we start freaking out a little bit. Yes, we know we can't take our money with us when we die, yet we still put such a high importance on having it to survive. With money, we feel confident—without it, we don't. At least, that's how we are here in the United States.

Interestingly enough, the Bible touches on this topic in the book of John. Mary, Lazarus' sister, owned a vial of an extremely expensive perfume called Spikenard. This bottle was worth a lot, and Mary did something bonkers—she poured the entire bottle onto Jesus' feet. She did this while weeping, worshipping, and drying His feet with her hair.

The people around her freaked out. How could she waste something that expensive? But to Mary, this wasn't a waste at all. She was so confident that she was in the presence of the Son of God that pouring out the entire bottle didn't scare her one bit. Little did they know, Jesus was about to be crucified, and this grand gesture was done in preparation for His burial. Mary knew that being in the presence of the Messiah was worth more than money could ever buy.

There is nothing wrong with wealth or using financial wisdom. However, that is not where our confidence comes from! The Lord is our provider, our rock, our greatest security. We must surrender our hearts, and our finances, to Jesus. Pursuing His presence brings a confidence that changes everything!

*God, possessions can't make me confident like You can. Thank You for providing me with a gift money could never buy. Amen.*

# Chasing Approval

*Obviously, I'm not trying to win the approval of people, but of God. If pleasing people were my goal, I would not be Christ's servant.*

**GALATIANS 1:10 NLT**

Growing up, I was blessed with some awesome friends. However, there was always part of me that wanted to win over those who *didn't* like me. I would go out of my way to be kind to these people, bring up things we had in common, or find excuses to spend time with them. My desire to please all people at all times consumed me—and sometimes this insecurity led to compromising who I was for the sake of being accepted. *(Good grief, desperate much? And I'm not even a politician!)*

Come to find out, my efforts were all in vain. No matter how hard I tried, these folks remained unpredictable, unkind, and consistently cruel. When I learned to let it go, I was able to see the beauty *(and the rarity)* of the lifelong friendships that were right in front of me. Thankfully, decades later, our sisterhood is still stuck like Gorilla Glue. Who knows, we'll probably arrange to live in the same retirement home as old ladies and party like it's 1999.

Sometimes we struggle with confidence simply because we aren't someone's cup of tea. We think that *if only they* liked us, *if only they* spoke kindly about us, we wouldn't be so insecure. Subliminally, this attitude places our confidence in the hands of people rather than placing it in the hands of Jesus.

While being friendly is something we must always pursue, we must never compromise who we are in Christ. Paul understood this concept very well in his letter to the Galatians. When we chase after the approval of people, we are not acting as Christ's servants. I'll even take it one step further and say this:

Chasing after approval can become an idol.

Why?

Because the chase is not about the Kingdom. It's about our ego!

Instead, we must actively chase after the approval of the One who strips our ego—fully and completely—and replaces it with a *holy confidence* instead.

I know that was a hard one to swallow. But I can guarantee you this—chasing after God's favor, not man's, will bring you a confidence that changes everything!

God, Your approval is all I need.
Remind me of that daily. Amen.

# Discipline Brings Confidence

*For the moment all discipline
seems painful rather than pleasant,
but later it yields the peaceful fruit
of righteousness to those
who have been trained by it.*
HEBREWS 12:11 ESV

Let's be honest—the word *discipline* has an exhausting vibe to it, doesn't it? We associate discipline with things like aggressive exercise, intense studying, or a good old-fashioned spanking. And none of those are fun *(I mean, unless you're a little coo-coo for cocoa puffs)*. Seriously, though, discipline is something we tend to run from. As a kid, I remember hiding behind a giant boy in our class to avoid getting caught laughing in chapel. In high school, I remember "conveniently" getting sick on the days we were scheduled to run laps at early morning practice. Facing consequences, and facing discomfort, simply goes against our nature.

However, walking in confidence is the byproduct of good discipline. When we discipline ourselves, we perform better. When we are disciplined by authority, we learn to do the right thing. When we practice a discipline, we become well-versed in certain branches of knowledge. This goes for every aspect of life—including our spiritual life.

Just as athletes physically train to be good at their sport, we must spiritually train to become more like Jesus. Spiritual discipline does so much good for the mind, body, and heart. It helps us to avoid apathy and insecurity, but it also allows us to carry ourselves with a special kind of confidence—the kind where people look at us and wonder what we have.

Praying, meditating, witnessing, Bible reading, and corporate worship are some examples of spiritual discipline—but there are deeper examples, too, like solitude and silence, which allow us to listen for God's voice amid the noise of everyday life. When we are aligned with God's purpose for our lives, we get to experience a love like no other. We want to walk in the ways He is showing us to walk, we want to see the things He is trying to show us, we want to respond in the ways He is calling us to. And when we do this, we are able to fully embrace the peace and joy of our Father. So while the word *discipline* is not a fun one, the experience of walking in the ways of Jesus comes with a full life with unimaginable possibilities.

> God, I want to be more disciplined, especially spiritually. Help me to delight in pursuing Your purposes for my life. Amen.

# The Most Important Devotion You'll Ever Read ...Again

*Now faith is the substance of things hoped for, the evidence of things not seen.*

HEBREWS 11:1 KJV

Dang, the fact that you've stuck with me for this long is pretty impressive. I haven't scared you away with my wacky words and my loud love for Jesus yet?! That's cool. Let's be besties. Better yet—let's become family. Yes, seriously! Anyone who surrenders their life to Christ steps into a family of believers right away!

We know we can confidently rely on Jesus. But we also can go one step further. Our confidence in Him is so great, that we have faith. We believe He is God, the Savior of the world, the only way to heaven—even though we have never seen Him with our natural eyes.

I'll tell you why I am so confident in my faith in Jesus. For one, God really likes to prove how real He is; therefore, the evidence of God's existence is loud—the complexity of creation, the wonder of nature, the miracle of life, and the written Word that explains it all in truthful detail. How awesome is our Creator!

I am also confident God sent His Son, Jesus, to die for my sins, because with every prophecy stated in the Old Testament concerning the Messiah, Jesus inarguably fulfilled—over, and over, and over again. All of this, every bit of it, is proof of His majesty and glory *(also, I highly recommend you check out* The Case for Christ *by former atheist Lee Strobel. Sums all of this up beautifully!)*

If you're unsure if heaven is where you'll end up, or if you're ready to leave the old you behind and become a new creation in Him, pray this prayer with me:

> Jesus, even though I've never seen You, I believe in You. I believe You are the Son of the One who created all things, including me. I believe He sent You to die instead of me, taking all my wrongdoings and shame with You, and You are alive today, and my decision to follow You allows me to be with You forever. Today, I surrender. Come into my life and use me for Your glory. Amen.

The evidence of God's existence is loud—the complexity of creation, the wonder of nature, the miracle of life, and the written Word that explains it all in truthful detail.

# Our Scars Are Our Witness

*Then he said to Thomas,*
*"Put your finger here, and see my hands;*
*and put out your hand,*
*and place it in my side.*
*Do not disbelieve, but believe."*
JOHN 20:27 ESV

I've got a scar on my left hand, and it's not cute. It happened when I was in diapers—my mom was making bows for my hair *(the large, giant, bigger-than-your-head, obnoxious kind, of course)*, and I pulled on the cord of the glue gun. The scalding-hot tip landed just below my index finger, and apparently the sight of the wound was faint-worthy. However, the doctor reassured my mom, "Don't worry, the scar will be gone by prom." Well, hate to break it to you, buddy, but I went to prom *thrice*, and that Nike-checkmark-looking thing is still there. Sometimes when I glance at it, my brain hears the tagline "Just Do It" in the voice of Morgan Freeman. Don't ask me why, it just fits so well in my quirky mind.

When I think of the word *scars*, I recall the story of Thomas, one of Jesus' disciples. This doubting dude didn't believe Jesus rose from the dead—after all, Thomas watched the crucifixion with his own two eyes. But when Thomas's eyes witnessed the evidence of the risen King, everything changed. Jesus used His scars as a witnessing tool, one that caused Thomas to go from an unbeliever to a believer.

We all carry scars, both physical and emotional. Sometimes we try to hide the evidence of what we've gone through, rather than confidently showing it as proof that we've been healed. A scar's intent is not to reopen the wound of suffering, it's to serve as a symbol of God's supernatural healing power!

Friend, the pain of your past is *nothing* to be ashamed of. Your scars are your testimony, and your testimony is your witness. Jesus wasn't afraid to show His scars, and neither should you! You have been healed by the risen King, and you have the evidence to prove it. May your scars instill within you a confidence that changes everything—confidence that you serve a Healer, and confidence that He will use your story as a tool to heal others too.

> God, I choose to see my scars
> as a reminder of healing rather
> than a reminder of pain. May my
> testimony lead others to You. Amen.

# Identity in Christ

*This means that anyone who belongs to Christ has become a new person. The old life is gone; a new life has begun!*
II CORINTHIANS 5:17 NLT

Life is full of confusing changes. One minute you have it all figured out, and then suddenly, you don't. Going from a big dawg eighth-grader to a teeny-weeny freshman was pretty jarring for my little identity. So were things like the end of a career, the loss of a relationship, or the applause of an accolade slowly fading into the past. Heck, even something as silly as a really bad haircut would make me lose myself sometimes.

As humans, we habitually attach ourselves to temporary things—jobs, relationships, titles, homes, awards, even appearances. And when those things are stripped away, we're left wondering, *Well, if I'm not that anymore, then who am I?*

I imagine Jesus felt the sting of change too—moving from glorious heaven to lame-o earth, shifting roles from a no-big-deal carpenter to the promised Messiah, going from beloved and worshipped to betrayed and crucified. Yet, even in all of that, His true identity never changed—He was *(and is)* the Alpha and the Omega, the beginning and the end, the same yesterday, today, and forever.

Identity is something we are all chasing. Everyone desires to belong, to understand themselves, or to live for something purposeful. This is not a bad thing—in fact, I believe God created us this way on purpose! He wants us to seek Him so we can find Him—because every answer in our quest for self-identification can be found in God's love for us.

However, in our world today, people are suffering more from identity confusion than ever before. This is the twisted work of the enemy, a desperate attempt to steer us further away from the truth. Satan knows that once we realize who we are—children of the Most High, bought with a price, chosen and free—he cannot win.

An identity rooted in Christ leaves no room for an identity crisis. The Word of God has been given to us as a lamp for our feet and a light for our path. Surrendering ourselves to Him, especially our identity, brings a confidence that changes everything!

> God, Your love for me is the root of my identity. Thank You for allowing me to walk in the light of being Your daughter. Amen.

# Calm, Cool, & Self-Controlled

*A man without self-control*
*is like a city broken into*
*and left without walls.*

PROVERBS 25:28 ESV

I've always been drawn to calm, cool, and collected people. There's peace in their presence, an effortless ease that makes you feel safe. My aunt Ann was one of those people. No matter what kind of existential crisis I was facing *(sometimes a serious issue, sometimes just my period),* she would always listen with such warmth and grace. Not only was she calm and cool, Aunt Ann was also very collected. She ate healthy, exercised, worked outside, spent time with the Lord, served the needy, and loved her family well. I never once saw her react poorly out of fear or insecurity. She was just all-around confident—you could see it, you could feel it. And I firmly believe that stemmed from one very important Fruit of the Spirit: *self-control.*

The Bible links self-control as a foundational trait for walking in confidence. There's a famous verse in II Timothy 1:7 (ESV) that says this:

> *"For God gave us a spirit not of fear but of power and love and self-control."*

Self-control is mentioned here. However, I memorized a different translation of this verse growing up. In many other Bible translations, the word *self-control* is replaced with the phrase *sound mind*. A sound mind, as defined in the dictionary, is one that is sane and rational. And in the Bible, a sound mind is defined as one that is alert, sober, and focused on the eternal hope we have in Jesus.

I've never thought of "a sound mind" as being interchangeable with "self-control," but it makes sense. When our mind is sound, our actions are sound, and when our actions are sound, our reactions are sound. Being of sound mind leads to wisdom, which leads us to always doing the right thing. Doing the right thing is a byproduct of self-control, and when we live righteously, it naturally leads to confidence!

A lack of self-control causes us to spiral with poor decisions and insecurity. However, the presence of self-control leads us to a confidence that changes everything. Calm, cool, and self-controlled is the best way to be!

*God, I want so badly to exhibit more self-control in my life. Help me to grow in this Fruit of the Spirit so I can walk confidently and with a sound mind. Amen.*

# Stop! Collaborate and Listen!

*Two are better than one,
because they have a good reward for their toil.
For if they fall, one will lift up his fellow.*
ECCLESIASTES 4:9-10 ESV

You didn't read that title—you rapped it, didn't you? Same here, girlfriend. How can you not? We're going to talk about collaboration today, so the title seemed fitting!

Learning to work with others is a life skill. In school, we're told to pick a buddy for certain lessons or exercises. In high school, we're assigned partners for projects. *(Even though it's usually the nerd who does all the work. I, indeed, was that nerd.)* Being that I'm now in the social media world, part of my job is to collaborate with brands. For them, working with me helps with their marketing, and for me, working with them helps me buy groceries.

God has given all of us different gifts. And when I think about the individual gifts we all have, I think of a box of matches. Each match, when lit individually, gives off an equal amount of light. However, if the matches are lit all together, the flame burns bigger and brighter. The same goes for us—our God-given talents are all equal in shine and warmth and importance. But when we collaborate with others, we can make an even greater difference for the kingdom of God.

In the Bible, God highlights the value of collaborative relationships. Moses didn't deliver the Israelites by himself; he needed his brother Aaron to speak on his behalf. Aaron was a great speaker; Moses was not. Now, could God have healed Moses' speech impediment in an instant? Of course. But doing something as massive as leading an entire people out of Egypt would have been pretty daunting to do alone, don't you think?

The purpose of collaboration is not to remind us of our weaknesses. Instead, it causes our strengths to operate at their fullest. If we want to perform better, live better, and serve better, we must be willing to collaborate with others! Working together allows the light of Jesus to shine bright in this topsy-turvy life!

*God, thank You for the gifts You've given me. Using them alongside the gifts of others brings a confidence that changes everything! Amen.*

# Be Bold

*I will praise You, L*ORD*, with all my heart;*
*I will tell of all the marvelous things*
*You have done.*
**PSALM 9:1 NLT**

We almost lost my sister at the river. She was only three years old, but that little booger thought she could impress her new friend by swimming like a mini Michael Phelps. While showing off her best doggy paddle, a current swept her underwater, and she got stuck. None of us saw it happen, but a nearby woman did. She ran toward our little daredevil, reached down, and started pulling. Thankfully, she was able to dislodge my goofy sister and yank her out of the water unharmed. To this day, we boldly talk about this story—even though it was quite traumatic, we can't contain our gratitude of how God used that woman to save my sister's life.

Sometimes we struggle to boldly share about our own salvation. We're afraid of sounding "preachy," or making others feel weird. Plus, if we don't have a bold personality, it feels much easier to leave the salvation messages up to the pastors.

I think what happens, too, is we get so comfortable in our daily lives that the urgency of sharing the Good News is minimal. We easily lose sight of how tomorrow isn't promised, and death's door is imminent. However, *when we fully understand* what Jesus did for us, *it's hard not to* tell others about Him!

If we want to ignite confidence in boldly sharing about Jesus, these ways can help:

1. *Read the Bible.* The more we learn, the harder it is to keep inside!
2. *Share personal testimonies.* This uplifts and encourages others!
3. *Consume faith-based media.* Watching things like *War Room* or *The Chosen* powerfully illustrates our Savior and reinvigorates our faith.
4. *Explore.* When we visit places that contain biblical history like museums, cathedrals, or even different countries, it connects us with Christ on a whole new level!

Boldness in sharing the Good News doesn't come from natural self-confidence. It comes from the assurance we have in Jesus. Ask the Holy Spirit to fill you with boldness and a confidence to share your faith story with others.

> God, I am unashamed of the gospel of Christ. Give me a chance to show that today. Amen.

# The Brightest in the Room

*For we are his workmanship,
created in Christ Jesus for good works,
which God prepared beforehand,
that we should walk in them.*

**EPHESIANS 2:10 ESV**

Have you ever walked into a room of people and thought, *Whoa, I certainly do not belong here!* The classy attire, beautiful faces, and poised personas seem way out of your league. You're wondering how you got invited to this fancy shindig in the first place, while also trying to hide an accidental Coca-Cola stain on your $28 Target dress.

In other rooms of people, you may think, *Whoa, I'm definitely not the sharpest tool in this shed!* The business verbiage, collegiate conversations, and well-educated dialects go far beyond your small-town-USA little brain. While they're chatting about the stock market, you're just trying to figure out what to do with your hands.

While we know comparison is the thief of joy, let's be real—sometimes the differences are so obvious, we just can't ignore them! But instead of hiding out in the bathroom all night, how can we approach these situations with confidence and purpose?

The answer is simple—*walk into every room like Jesus sent you.* Yes, even in rooms like this. Regardless of your background, social status, or education level, God has an assignment upon your life—and that assignment *will* send you into rooms of people who aren't your people!

God doesn't send us into unusual crowds to make us feel inferior. He might do it, however, for the purpose of fulfilling His ultimate plan for our lives. Not being the most admired person in the room *gives us room*—it gives us room to learn, to grow, to observe, and to glean. Other times, the purpose of our presence in that room isn't for our gain at all. *Maybe the Lord wants us to make someone else feel seen and admired, even if we don't feel seen and admired ourselves!*

Despite what our carnal eyes perceive, the brightest person in the room isn't always the prettiest, smartest, or wealthiest. Instead, the brightest person in the room is the one who walks in willful obedience, humble selflessness, and joyful readiness. May you confidently shine that light of Jesus in every room you go!

> God, I choose to go into any room
> You need, even if it's far beyond
> my comfort zone. I trust Your will
> for my life completely. Amen.

# The New Kid on the Block

*An intelligent heart acquires knowledge,*
*and the ear of the wise seeks knowledge.*

**PROVERBS 18:15 ESV**

One of the most confident people I know is my stepdad, Bob. His confidence is not the arrogant, know-it-all type—but the steady, capable type. No matter what kind of social situation we are in, Bob can *absolutely thrive* while still remaining true to his character. I'll never forget the first time he hung out with us when he started dating our mom. We were loud, uninhibited, sharing inside jokes he was oblivious to and recounting memories he wasn't there for. However, none of it moved him—Bob was a joyful observer and a thoughtful engager. I'm sure we didn't make it easy on him that first night, but it didn't matter—his confidence made it easy on himself.

Being the new kid on the block *(work, school, church, friendships, or blended families)* can always present its challenges. Finding space to belong in an already established environment can feel sensitive and awkward. I can only imagine Ruth felt this same way—she was new to the town of Bethlehem, new to the Jewish religion, new to being a widow, and new to the working class. Nothing around her was familiar, and she delicately tried to find a way to survive. However, *because she confidently chose to adjust with joy and without complaint,* God honored her. Boaz, a wealthy businessman, fell madly in love with her—and their marriage was part of the lineage of Christ. Talk about redemption!

In order for us to walk in confidence when approaching a new season or territory, there are three qualities both my stepdad Bob and Ruth from the Bible exhibited beautifully:

1. *Joyful observation.* Be okay with being an observer! Enjoy learning about new people or new surroundings without allowing insecurity or FOMO to take over.
2. *Thoughtful engagement.* Be curious! Ask questions, gain wisdom, get to know those around you. Confidence is gained by a thoughtful, others-focused approach.
3. *Unwavering trust.* Even if fitting in is taking longer than expected, don't let it affect your attitude! Trust the Lord—He will allow everything to gel in ways you never imagined.

New seasons can be blessed seasons. Embrace them, and walk in a confidence that changes everything!

> God, in every new season, let me embrace it joyfully, thoughtfully, selflessly, and confidently! Amen.

# The Ultimate Trust Fall

*But blessed is the one who trusts in the Lord,*
*whose confidence is in Him.*

JEREMIAH 17:7 NIV

There's a humorous "trust fall trend" going around on Instagram and TikTok. One person leans backward expecting to be caught, but the "catcher" suddenly steps out of the way to speak into the camera. This causes their "falling friend" to dramatically drop on the floor *(but don't worry, they land on something soft out of the frame)*. It frightens viewers at first, but once they realize it's fake, it's funny. This trend has become a catchy way to market a message, albeit shocking. Oh, the things people will do nowadays to go viral!

I've never enjoyed trust falls myself because of that very thing: What if they drop me? What if I'm too heavy? What if I *die*? Thanks, but no thanks. I'd rather show my trust in normal ways without potentially breaking a vertebra.

Sometimes our walk with the Lord feels very similar to a trust fall. We can't physically see Him, we feel uneasy and afraid, and we don't know how things will end up. However, unlike flawed people, Jesus will *never* allow us to fall. He will never be too weak to carry our many burdens. He will never trick us into thinking He'll protect us, only to watch us stumble. We're reminded of this in Romans 3:3-4 (NLT), which says:

*"True, some of them were unfaithful; but just because they were unfaithful, does that mean God will be unfaithful? Of course not! Even if everyone else is a liar, God is true."*

The key to a confident life is a fearless life, and the secret to confidence is taking God at His word. Every single thing He says is true. His yes is yes, His no is no—if He says it, we can believe it!

It's easy to feel confident in someone when you know how much they love you. Even though it's hard to fathom, God loves you *way more* than your parents, spouse, children, or friends do. He is the definition of love—and because He loves you like this, you've got no reason to fear.

Take the ultimate trust fall into the arms of Jesus—it will lead to a confidence that changes everything!

**God, I trust You.**
**Your love will never cause me to stumble.**
**Thank You for that. Amen.**

# The Ingredients List

*But what comes out of the mouth
proceeds from the heart,
and this defiles a person.*

MATTHEW 15:18 ESV

In my young adult years, I never cared to check the ingredients list on certain foods or beverages. If it looked good, sounded good, or tasted good, I bought it—regardless of what it consisted of. However, now that I'm a mom, things are very different. No matter how it looks, sounds, or tastes, it better be nutritious and free from that little demon known as red dye 40. Now, do I sometimes cave and allow my children to have the occasional bag of gas-station Doritos? Of course. However, then I'm usually having to deal with two hyperactive Tasmanian devils spiraling out of control for about a thirty-minute period *(boy oh boy, help me, Lord. At least they're cute, right?)*

The purpose of an ingredients list is to specify the contents inside a package, giving us a clearer idea of what we're choosing to consume. Good ingredients improve our health and reflect well for us on the outside, but poor ingredients damage our health and reflect badly for us on the outside.

This same idea applies to us in our journey toward

confidence. Ingredients matter—not only physically but spiritually. Like it or not, our outward appearance, including our actions and attitudes, can often reflect our inner state. Healthy choices—whether in food, actions, or mindset—can contribute to our well-being.

If we aspire to cultivate a confident and fulfilling life, we must consider our internal ingredients. When it comes to our spiritual diet specifically, the healthiest ingredients we can include are the Fruits of the Spirit: love, joy, peace, patience, kindness, goodness, faithfulness, gentleness, and self-control. In order to maintain these healthy ingredients and prevent them from decaying, we must feast our eyes on Scripture. We must also spend quality time with Jesus, with other believers, and with godly influences. Doing this will allow our thoughts, words, and actions to display a healthy, confident life!

> God, I want to be more conscious about my ingredients list. Help me to be nutritious in my diet, actions, and character. Amen.

# Presence over Platform

*Commit to the LORD whatever you do,*
*and He will establish your plans.*

PROVERBS 16:3 NIV

My mom is not a celebrity, but one time I thought she was. We were visiting my grandparents for the holidays and decided to go have a no-big-deal lunch at Chili's. Our waitress approached—but when she saw my mom, she about passed out. Fan-girling so hard, this woman said: *"Starla! You were always my idol when we were in high school! Oh my gosh! Can you sign my napkin?!"* We graciously laughed even though it felt like a joke, but I can assure you, this lady was one hundred percent sincere. My mom was extremely kind, even talked to her about Jesus for a bit. However, we ate and left a little faster than normal.

As humans, we tend to idolize those with platforms. Sometimes we put these people on a pedestal and see them as superhuman; other times we glare at them, wondering how they got so "lucky" when we didn't. Or, because platforms appear glamorous, we start desperately chasing after one of our own. We think, *Man, if I can just gain something similar to what she has, I'd be confident!*

Most of us weren't born into a billionaire family, don't

own a big business, and don't have millions of followers. However, despite popular opinion, success is not defined by what we have or what we've accomplished; it's defined by *our faithfulness to God's calling*. A life of success here on earth is a life of constant alignment with the presence of God.

If we want a confidence that changes everything, we need to stop chasing the platform and start chasing His presence. When we strive daily to seek His face, it leads us on a path toward godly wisdom, which will open doors of opportunity that we could have never opened ourselves.

Jesus can only shine through us in public if we spend time with Him in private. And today's verse, Proverbs 16:3, gives us a simple blueprint for a life of success. His presence will always be better than a platform—and it's His presence alone that brings a confidence that changes everything!

> God, all I want is You.
> The shiny things of this world
> can't compare to spending my life
> in relationship with You. Amen.

When we strive daily to seek His face, it leads us on a path toward godly wisdom, which will open doors of opportunity that we could have never opened ourselves.

# The Struggle Is Real

*Being confident of this,
that He who began a good work in you
will carry it on to completion
until the day of Christ Jesus.*

**PHILIPPIANS 1:6 NIV**

Has anyone ever asked you how you were doing, but you habitually responded with *"I'm doing good!"* even though you weren't? It didn't feel appropriate to spill your truthful guts: *"No, Susan, I'm actually not okay. My life is chaos, work is awful, my marriage is as stale as old bread, and I've gained seventeen pounds. How are you, though? I saw on Facebook how you ran another marathon—that was what, your tenth one this year?"* (Insert hard eye roll.)

While others appear to be stable and thriving, sometimes our life feels like a magnet for new problems—physical, relational, emotional, or financial. It's difficult to reject self-absorption and self-pity during these seasons, and the idea of walking in confidence is seemingly laughable. So, how on earth can we keep our head above water when we're sinking inside a struggle bus surrounded by empty juice boxes, sticky floorboards, and tear-stained seats?

First of all, we live in a fix-it-now society. We'd rather

not face our struggles head-on because it's too hard, too complex, and it takes too long. Instead, we do things to feel better quickly—like masking the pain with denial or deflecting the blame by finger-pointing. However, this isn't making us more resilient—it's making us *weaker*.

Growth in life requires us to go the long way. It requires us to seek biblical truth, receive godly wisdom, and embrace self-reflection. This allows us to learn through the struggle, without allowing the struggle to control our next steps.

Here's the other thing—despite how it feels, *trials are not a curse, they are an opportunity!* Paul's life was a vivid model of this. He chose perseverance instead of pity, purpose instead of paralysis. Following this example allows the light of Jesus to shine through us, even in the midst of harrowing difficulty.

Struggle is the most important part of our journey—it's the foundation that builds our character, resilience, and confidence. Oh, friend, you're not alone in this! Allow the Holy Spirit to comfort you, lead you, and refine you. He brings a confidence that changes everything!

> **God, a life of continuous struggle isn't my portion. I desire a healing that is full, honest, and complete. Amen.**

# Your Circle Matters

*Do not be misled:*
*"Bad company corrupts good character."*
1 CORINTHIANS 15:33 NIV

The most popular fruit we buy in our house is strawberries. It's our daughter's favorite, and one of the only "healthy snacks" my picky-eating boy will agree to. However, you've got to eat them quickly—because when one goes bad, they all go bad. One day they are red and fresh, the next day they are fuzzy like an old man's chest—all because one strawberry just couldn't keep it together.

Sometimes a huge reason why we struggle with confidence is due to the company we keep. The fact is simple—bad company corrupts good character. This is especially difficult when these relationships are close-knit—friends, coworkers, extended family members. It's hard to know how to safely audit your circle without fear of being called judgmental, hateful, or "too good."

However, let me encourage you with this truth—it is okay to pivot with grace for the sake of personal growth. It is okay to focus on fruitful friendships rather than tiptoeing around insecure ones. It's also okay to love people from afar in their current season, while choosing not to stay in that same season yourself. Sometimes we stick around in certain relationships just to keep the peace—however, being a peacemaker also looks like setting boundaries and knowing when it's time to gracefully step in another direction.

Just as we can identify a tree by its fruit, we can identify a person by their actions. If you want to know if someone is good for your growth, look at their life. Do they make wise choices, socially and financially? Do they have healthy relationships, personally and professionally? Do they display good character, emotionally and spiritually?

Now, obviously, every situation is different. Sometimes the splinter in their eye isn't the problem, it's the log in our own. We must take an honest look at ourselves—are we good for the circle of others? Are we displaying a character that reflects good, healthy fruit?

The pursuit of growth, within our circle and within ourselves, is vital for a fruitful life. Doing this brings a confidence that changes everything!

> God, I want a fruitful circle,
> and I want to be a fruitful part
> in the circle of others. Help me to
> pivot with grace, in my relationships
> and in my own life. Amen.

# Zip It!

*A perverse person stirs up conflict,
and a gossip separates close friends.*
**PROVERBS 16:28 NIV**

People *never* gossip in the Christian world, right? How preposterous to even suggest such a thing! Bible-believin' and Jesus-lovin' women would *never*, could *never*! Instead, every juicy detail is prefaced with "I'm just letting y'all know so you can pray," wrapped up in a pretty "bless their heart" bow. It's not gossip, it's just another thing to add to the intercession list! *Right?*

While that was supposed to be funny, it might've struck a chord! Maybe you've been the victim of said "prayer requests," or maybe you've engaged in them yourself. The truth is—most likely—we've all been on both sides of this coin.

But here's the deal—the more we mature in our personal relationship with Jesus, the scarier gossip becomes. It heightens our sensitivity and fear of the Lord, causing us to think before we weaponize our tongues. *And believe it or not, this leads to confidence*—and I'll tell you why:

When we resist in sharing about people's misfortunes, we honor God.

When we resist in speaking against people *(even if they've hurt us)*, we honor God.

The more we honor God with our tongues, the more

protection and favor we receive. And when we feel protected and favored in life, we feel confident—don't we?

A recent quote by a famous pastor says it best:

*"I don't gossip about people because I fear Jesus in them. I fear I would speak badly about someone so valued by God that Jesus died for them. I fear I would portray them as something less valuable than that. I fear how God would deal with me if I betrayed the people made in His image."*

That hits hard, doesn't it? The fact is, gossip is damaging, bridge-burning, and petty—but we simply cannot hang with petty if we want to walk in purpose. Obviously, we will come across people we don't jive with, and that's okay. However, they are no less valuable in the sight of God than we are, and our tongues should reflect that!

We are called to build others up with our words, *especially* behind their backs. This kind of self-control brings a confidence that changes everything!

> God, give me a check in my spirit before I attempt to speak negatively about others. Amen.

# That's Totally About Me!

*Good sense makes one slow to anger,
and it is his glory to overlook an offense.*
**PROVERBS 19:11 ESV**

In simpler times, if a bully didn't like you, they were in-your-face about it—boldly telling you, unashamedly telling others, or slapping you around like Biff from *Back to the Future*. But now that we have the internet, the trolls have emerged from their caves—no longer living under a bridge but happily living behind a keyboard. Between passive-aggressive posts, elusive comments, or "vague-booking," the presence of online discord and drama is a dime a dozen.

The enemy has done a fantastic job with cyberbullying—destroying relationships and ripping people apart. However, Satan has also created another trap—one where people receive every post as a personal diss. Because of this, the body of Christ today is walking in offense *way more* than they walk in confidence, *and the enemy loves it*.

Cyberbullying inflicts a searing, indescribable pain—but we must ask the Lord to heal us from these wounds. Otherwise, discernment is replaced with a rabbit-hole-like paranoia, and that won't produce God's best for our lives! Instead of inserting our insecurities into everything that is said, posted, or insinuated, we must actively take our thoughts captive. Sure, there might be someone who isn't our biggest fan, but take heart. More than likely, that person's world doesn't revolve entirely around their dislike for you!

However, I am realistic. I know that hurt people hurt people—and sometimes online jabs are intentional and personal. In this case, you have two options:

1. *Approach it!* Use the Matthew 18:15 method. Go directly to the person who is presumably bashing you—but in a rational, calm, self-controlled manner.
2. *Ignore it!* Proverbs 19:11 beautifully exemplifies this. Overlooking an offense and keeping your heart pure can eventually lead to vindication and restoration.

The enemy wants to use us as puppets in his twisted little show. He wants you to "vent" online with pointed posts and indirect jabs, stirring discord and burning bridges. He wants you to take everything personally, walking in offense instead of walking in confidence. However, we must rise above this! Online and in person, let us walk in maturity and harmony with one another. Doing this creates a confidence that changes everything!

> God, give me discernment and wisdom before I read (or post) anything online. Amen.

# Am I an Imposter?

*Even before He made the world,*
*God loved us and chose us in Christ*
*to be holy and without fault in His eyes.*
**EPHESIANS 1:4 NLT**

I'll never forget the time I was invited to hang with a group of "cool girls" in high school. They were older, popular, beautiful, funny, and *such a blast*—so receiving this invitation was a dream come true. However, it was also highly nerve-wracking. I thought for sure they'd regret inviting me: *"Wow, we didn't realize Hannah was so weird. Why is she breaking out so badly on her forehead? What a strange outfit choice. Is it me, or did she just eat a bag of Funyuns? She's not as cool as I expected. Whose idea was it to invite her, anyway?"* The anxiety was astronomical—but the hangout itself turned out to be completely fine. I walked away wondering why I'd worked myself up so much. They were normal girls, just like me!

*Imposter syndrome* is the internal belief that you are not as competent as others perceive you to be. Simply put, it's when you feel phony or fraudulent—that you're not qualified enough to deserve the blessing, that success was only by happenstance, or that others will expose your inadequacies. The anxiety of this can be crippling, leading to a lack of confidence altogether.

If you, too, have struggled with this, I have one question for you:

*Do you believe these feelings come from the Lord?*

No! They don't! Imposter syndrome tries to suppress your influence as a friend, leader, and child of the Most High—and that does *not* come from the Holy Spirit!

To overcome imposter syndrome for good, try these things:

1. Stop placing your identity around who you *think* you are, and start forming your identity around *Whose* you are!
2. Read the Word daily—it supernaturally corrects the way you think!
3. Choose worship over worry and praise over presumptions!
4. Ask God for healing, wisdom, and confidence!

Imposter syndrome is stealing from us—our calling, our blessings, our joy. But not today, Satan! May you walk in a confidence that changes everything, knowing your inheritance and identity come from the God Who made the heavens and the earth!

*God, help me to grow in wisdom, so I can gain confident hope in Who You are and how much You love me. Amen.*

# Don't Walk on Water...Yet

*Behold, I will bring to it health and healing,
and I will heal them and reveal to them
abundance of prosperity and security.*
JEREMIAH 33:6 ESV

When I think of confident people in the Bible, I think of my homie Peter. That dude's personality exuded total confidence: leader-like, ambitious, one of Jesus' favorites. Yet, Peter is also known for his massive fails. He saw himself as loyal, yet he angrily sliced a guy's ear off like some sort of samurai. He considered himself the greatest disciple, yet he denied Jesus three times. (And ironically, his "chickening out" moment was followed by a loud *cock-a-doodle-doo*.) And famously, he sunk like a sack of potatoes while trying to walk on water. Peter is a prime example of displaying confidence on the outside while being very unstable on the inside.

Like Peter, there are parts of us that are still weak and broken. Sometimes it's hard to admit this, because we are so eager to move on with confidence and do the next big thing. However, we must not deny the importance of acknowledging our struggles and allowing God to work in our weaknesses, for it is in our vulnerability that His strength is made perfect, and we can truly experience His grace and healing. Otherwise, we may end up in cock-a-doodle-doo-like situations, cutting people up in the process and foolishly sinking in our own sin.

God isn't always calling us to walk on water; sometimes He's calling us to stay in the boat. And that's okay! If we desire to walk confidently in His plan for our life, we must say yes to healing and refinement. This could look like facing our issues rather than making excuses or pretending they don't exist. This could look like feeling the roller coaster of emotions, strapped in with arms raised high in holy surrender. This could look like replacing every trauma and offense with grace and forgiveness, laying the pain of the past down so that we can embrace the healing and new life that God offers, allowing His love to transform our hearts and guide us toward a future filled with hope and purpose.

The more we allow the Lord to heal us, the more confident in Christ we will become. Maybe it's not time to walk on water. . .yet. But remember this: the boat is not where you're supposed to stay. Let God restore your heart, and confidently step out onto the water when He calls your name.

*God, make my heart brand-new. I don't want to stay in this cycle of brokenness; I want to become a new creation, one that is whole and healed and confident in You. Amen.*

# He Goes Before You

*The Lord went ahead of them.
He guided them during the day
with a pillar of cloud, and He provided
light at night with a pillar of fire.
This allowed them to travel
by day or by night.*
EXODUS 13:21 NLT

There was a time in our life when my husband, Blaine, and I were completely unsure of our next steps. We were newly married, he unexpectedly lost his job, and I wasn't finding any luck in the job search myself. Not knowing our next steps was extremely disconcerting, making it difficult for us to enjoy our marriage during this season of financial limbo.

However, God is known for doing cool little "God things"—and He began to clearly direct our steps. The Lord provided us with temporary jobs that kept us afloat, He sent us even better opportunities a few years down the road, and today we are both working in the fields we love. Not only that, our marriage today *(despite its twists and turns)* is more fun than we could've ever imagined! Even after two kids and a whole lot of life scenarios in between, I still think my man is a cutie patootie McBeauty little dude-y.

When Moses was leading the Israelites out of Egypt, I'm sure they were feeling the same way. Worried about the unknown and disconcerted with leaving their old life behind, they had no idea what would happen next. However, God went before them—He physically guided them every night and day, and all they had to do was trust His direction. Sure enough, God led the Israelites down a detoured path that protected them from harm and cleared the way for a life of freedom.

It's hard to feel secure and confident when your world gets shaken up. But even when you can't see what the future holds, the *Lord is already there*! He goes before you, clearing every obstacle. He is one step ahead, making your next moves safe. *God is already holding your tomorrow*—and since He is for you, who can be against you?

Take heart knowing that in every shift and change and detour of your life, *there ain't no way* He'll let you travel blindly! He is clearing your pathway forward—and that brings a confidence that changes everything!

> God, thank You for
> going before me. I trust You and
> will follow Your lead. Amen.

# The Road to Repentance

*All must repent of their sins and turn to God—
and prove they have changed
by the good things they do.*

ACTS 26:20 NLT

The most insecure I've ever felt in my life was when I was intentionally living in sin. You see, I was acting in a manner that went against God's best for my life and character, and in doing so, I was creating a barrier between myself and my loving Father. I knew certain things were wrong in God's eyes, but I did them anyway *(red flag number one)*. To numb the conviction that stirred in my heart, I convinced myself I was still a "good person" since I wasn't committing any crimes *(red flag number two)*. However, because I was constantly excusing my lifestyle, I refused to honestly admit that my lifestyle was the reason why I was so dang miserable *(red flag number three)*.

You might be thinking, *Geez, what's wrong with her? Who in their right mind intentionally lives in sin yet still calls themselves a Christian?* And to that, you're right. It's kind of like being a "Christian atheist," a person who believes in God but flippantly lives their life as if He doesn't exist. However, *if* that was your initial thought, I would also challenge you with this: even if your sins aren't intentionally lawbreaking and blatant, more than likely you've been guilty of intentionally living out subtle sins—ones like ridiculing, complaining, envying, being angry, gossiping, being stubborn, or being unforgiving. We like to make excuses for these subtle sins—pointing the finger at others, dismissing them nonchalantly, or even denying them altogether. However, regardless of its caliber, even the slightest presence of sin will keep us on a merry-go-round of misery.

When Paul preached the Good News to the Jews and Gentiles, he stressed the topic of repentance. Repentance is not only an expression of remorse, it is a complete turn in the opposite direction. God's grace covers us when we repent—however, grace doesn't mean we can still do whatever we want. *Grace is an undeserved chance to identify our waywardness and to leave it behind, for good!*

Let's remember the three red flags: *intentional sin, constant excuses, and prideful denial.* If these are present in our lives, then by golly, that's why we're struggling so much! Thankfully, the road to repentance is also a road to confidence. Purifying our hearts and doing a hard reset on our lifestyle is exactly what we need!

> God, help me identify the sin
> in my life and turn from it
> for good. Amen.

# Spiritual Vitality

*You thrill me, L*ORD*, with all You have done for me!*
*I sing for joy because of what You have done.*
PSALM 92:4 NLT

I've written about my aunt Ann a bunch, probably because her character was the closest to Jesus out of anyone I've ever known. Her age caused her to decline—but despite the frailness of her body and the loss of her memory, it didn't dampen her spirit. She still laughed and cracked jokes *(even if they didn't make any sense)*, she still told us how much she loved us *(even if she didn't know who we were anymore)*, and she still made cute old-lady-Southern-twang comments like "Well, praise the Lord!" *(even if she didn't have a reason to)*. There was an inherent strength about her, a light behind those cataract-filled eyes that never stopped shining. Even on her deathbed, she looked up at the ceiling and joyfully said, "Oh, if you can only see what I just saw!" How can someone that close to death seem so—alive?

The reason was simple: Aunt Ann remained vibrant until her last breath because of one thing: spiritual vitality. Jesus transformed her spiritually, and it shined through her physically. Reading the Word does this; thinking of others before ourselves does this; staying in community with believers does this; and living in a constant state of joy and gratitude does this.

When the Holy Spirit shines through us, three things happen:

1. *A joyful countenance.* When we intentionally recall all that God has done for us, we can't help but display a worshipful, grateful, and joyful attitude!
2. *Relational harmony.* The more spiritual vitality we have, the more love we have for others. The love God has for us starts to overflow in our relationships, producing greater unity than ever before!
3. *Personal growth.* Despite the aging of our physical bodies, spiritual vitality nourishes and transforms our souls. It prunes our personality, which results in unusual favor with both God and man!

We weren't created to walk around like zombies, depressed and bitter and annoyed all the time! We were created to *live* while we're alive! Spiritual vitality brings a confidence that changes everything—and yes, I mean everything!

> God, I know that spiritual vitality leads to a rich and satisfying life. Help me to have a worshipful attitude and relational harmony as I continue to grow in You. Amen.

# The Confidence Language

*"For in Him we live and
move and have our being."
As some of your own poets have said,
"We are His offspring."*

**ACTS 17:28 NIV**

Since I grew up on the border of Texas and Mexico, knowing a little Spanish was a part of the culture. However, some people coasted through life in our hometown without learning a lick of *español*—case in point, my husband. He will tell you, though, that if he simply put a little effort into it, he would have been "so fluent." *Right, buddy. Right.*

Just like grasping a new language, confidence works the same way—it's not something we are born with, it's something we learn over time. When we master skills, overcome obstacles, and develop meaningful relationships, it boosts our confidence—but all of that requires us to put in *just a little bit of effort.* However, life will knock us on our heinie, causing our confidence to fall with it sometimes. Comparison creeps into our minds, introversion latches onto our personalities, and isolation feels safer than facing wretched people. However, the Lord wants us to live, move, and exist as vessels and messagers for Him—and yes, that means we've got to face this big, bad, mean world sometimes!

No matter how badly we've been burned in the past, we can choose to walk in a God-centered confidence—including in our interpersonal skills! It's important for us to put *just a little bit of effort* into confident body language, and here are some ways to do that:

1. *Eye contact.* We serve a God who sees us through the eyes of grace, and we need to do the same for others. Eye contact makes people feel seen, wanted, and known.
2. *Chin up, shoulders back.* Posture is everything! An upright presence is a confident presence; it shows that you are a victor and not a victim, an overcomer who walks in joy and peace.
3. *Smile.* It's science—smiling is attractive. It establishes trust and builds relationships. There is power behind a smile—and guess what? The world needs yours!

You are not too far gone to walk in a confidence that changes everything. This journey is one that is learned—and one that will allow you to shine bright in this topsy-turvy life!

> God, I want to walk with a confident, encouraging presence. May I be a pleasant representation of You. Amen.

Confidence isn't about discovering what makes you *you*, it's about discovering the God who made you.

# Faith Is Confidence

*Now faith is confidence in what we hope for and assurance about what we do not see.*

HEBREWS 11:1 NIV

You've got your friends, you've got your besties, but then you have your *family friends*. These people are basically friends on steroids—you grow up with them, you vacation with them, you walk through hard things with them, you even share a sense of humor with them. That's how it is with Taylor—our families are basically related *(even though we're not)*, so quite frankly, she's just another sister to me. And coming from the most unbiased place as I possibly can, *Taylor is special*. If anyone exudes confidence, it's her. Not only has she always been so beautiful, accomplished, and well-liked, Taylor's entire character is immersed in her faith in Jesus. So, when she chose to name her firstborn daughter *Faith*, it made perfect sense!

Here's a fun fact about the word *faith*—you might not know this, but *faith is the equivalent to confidence*. The dictionary defines faith as "complete trust or confidence in someone or something," and confidence is defined as "the feeling or belief that one can rely on someone or something;

firm trust." The two words are a lot like family friends— basically related, even though they're not.

If we want to walk with a confidence that changes everything, it starts with faith. However, not just *any* faith. For example, I have faith that my house won't collapse—but a tornado can change that. I have faith that my car will start—but a dead battery can change that. I have faith that my husband loves me—but me developing a severe case of halitosis can change that *(I'm joking, guys. . .I think).*

Faith allows us to place our confidence in things unseen. But most of the time, these things can be temporary, conditional, or unreliable. The wonderful thing about Jesus, though, is He is *eternal*. His love is *unconditional*. His goodness is *never-changing*. Therefore, if we want to shine bright in this topsy-turvy life, it all starts with *faith in Jesus.*

God is closer, and more reliable, than any family friend. What an honor to be loved, chosen, and called as His own!

God, my confidence begins
and ends with You. I believe in You,
even though I cannot see You. I'm
confident that You will always love
me no matter what. Amen.

# A Reputation Above Reproach

*Therefore an overseer must be above reproach, the husband of one wife, sober-minded, self-controlled, respectable, hospitable, able to teach, not a drunkard, not violent but gentle, not quarrelsome, not a lover of money.*
1 TIMOTHY 3:2-3 ESV

That saying "What people think of you is none of your business" is very helpful when combatting people-pleasing insecurities. And gosh, I wish someone had told me that years ago! Because if people didn't like me, I *absolutely* made it my business. I'd stand there like a deer in headlights, wide-eyed and with heart-pounding anxiety if I wasn't everyone's cup of tea.

However, that's life. No matter how hard we try, there will be some people we can never please. No matter how kind we are, there will be some people who go out of their way to speak hatefully against us. We should never lose sleep over people's petty perceptions—however, there is a flip side to this. If we are constantly experiencing reputation problems, it might be time to take a deep breath and grab the magnifying glass.

When we surround ourselves with believers, it's like iron

sharpening iron. Godly friends will love us enough to tell us the truth and call us out on our wrongdoings. But instead of digging in our heels in pride, we must be teachable enough to listen. A reputation above reproach can't happen without a little humility—so it is very important for us to be honest, pliable, receptive, and willing to adhere to correction. This is a good thing—and a way for us to be a better example for Christ.

No, Jesus wasn't loved by all, but His reputation spoke for itself. Our job is to follow His example. The goal isn't to put our godliness on display or to be liked by everyone—it's to live with a clear conscience before God and man.

It's true, our character matters, our words matter, and our deeds matter. If we are able to embody Christ's love in our interactions, we can inspire others. Even if others seek to damage our reputation, it will be our track record of integrity that will always be our best defense. By living out our values with authenticity, we can bypass any man-made accusations to make meaningful impacts in the lives of others and glorify God in all we do.

> God, I know a good reputation in Your sight is more valuable than man's perception of me. Refine my character and keep me humble. Amen.

# Nobody Understands!

*Since He Himself
has gone through suffering and testing,
He is able to help us when we are being tested.*

**HEBREWS 2:18 NLT**

"Mom, you *just don't understand!*" My preteen daughter says this phrase emphatically, letting me know that I'm *way too old* to get it and *way too out of touch* to relate. She's right, there are things I don't understand for sure—words like *bruh* and *cap* and *rizz* are far beyond my vocabulary skills. I much prefer slang like *dude* and *cool* and *bye, Felicia,* thank you very much!

However, in every other area of life, I understand where she's coming from perfectly. I understand how hard it is to walk through puberty. I understand how challenging it is to juggle school and friends and extracurriculars and annoying siblings. Heck, I even understand why she believes her mom *just doesn't understand*.

How often do we assume that our heavenly Father *just doesn't understand* when we go through hard things? This difficult life is constantly throwing curveballs that break our spirit and destroy our confidence—something God Himself *surely* can't relate to, right? After all, He's just sitting up there, living in perfect heaven, surrounded by glory and unaffected by the fiery darts of the enemy. Must be nice!

But *this*, my friends, *this is exactly* why Jesus came—so He can understand what we're going through perfectly. Our every hurt, our every temptation, our every challenge, our every curveball—He understands. He went through it here on earth, and He received the rest of that pain on the cross. It's so easy for us to view Jesus as divine and holy and untouchable, but it's so important for us to acknowledge His humanity. He lived and suffered through a human life; therefore, He understands our life of suffering too.

When I sit my daughter down and explain how I went through similar things as a preteen, it helps her feel seen and not so alone. The Lord wants to do this for us too. The Bible is full of experiences that Jesus went through, ones that parallel our lives perfectly. Because He gets it, He can help us through it—and that brings us a confidence that changes everything!

> God, thank You for understanding me.
> I don't want self-pity to block me from
> living a confident life. Guide me and comfort
> me through every curveball. Amen.

# Candle Burning at Both Ends

*"This is not good!"*
*Moses' father-in-law exclaimed.*
*"You're going to wear yourself out—*
*and the people, too. This job is too heavy*
*a burden for you to handle all by yourself."*
**EXODUS 18:17-18 NLT**

Anyone else have a bad habit of biting off more than they can chew? It's like the whole world is sitting on our shoulders, as if we have no choice but to do it all by our lonesome selves *(insert sad violin music here)*. We do every chore ourselves *(because no one can do it like us)*. We take on additional responsibilities *(because we don't want to be "that girl" who inconveniences people)*. We try to juggle all the hats *(because we're afraid of the whining and the eye rolls and the sighs if we ask for help)*.

In this case, it's not self-confidence we lack. We know good 'n well we are *perfectly capable* of doing it all ourselves. However, when we overstretch our confidence like this, we become like a candle burning at both ends—which leaves us overstimulated, overcommitted, overshot, and overwhelmed.

Moses was just like this. He was assigned to be God's

messenger, but the responsibility of that made him feel like he had to do everything on his own—including mediating petty arguments and surface-level squabbles between the Israelites. That was until his father-in-law Jethro stepped in and said, "Dude, are you nuts? You can't handle every little problem by yourself! You're going to wear yourself out!"

Jethro encouraged Moses to equip, empower, and entrust leadership into the hands of other capable, God-fearing Israelites. If those leaders could just handle the smaller things, it would allow Moses the time and energy to handle the bigger things.

We must stop being so afraid to release control! Even if teaching or training isn't our strong suit, doing this will save us so much time and energy in the long run. Good leaders take the time to equip, empower, and entrust others to become capable leaders themselves. When we have help, it increases our productivity, rest, and success—and that, my friend, results in a confidence that changes everything.

*God, help me to equip, empower, and entrust others to help me when I need it. Amen.*

# Just My Luck!

*We make our own decisions,
but the Lord alone determines what happens.*

PROVERBS 16:33 CEV

I love card games, especially around the table with friends and family. However, sometimes my little blonde brain can't keep up. I often find myself perplexingly staring at my cards, counting out loud like a first grader, trying to determine my next move. However, while there is a level of skill, most card games are usually left up to chance—and when the chances don't align in our favor, it leaves us feeling frustrated and annoyed.

In life, sometimes we look at the hand we're dealt and think, *That's just my luck! Why can't I be on a winning streak like her? Why wasn't I born with better cards? Why do unfortunate things happen to me, while others are fine?*

The truth is, we don't know why things happen the way they do. However, if we want to walk in a confidence that changes everything, we must know that God is all-powerful, all-knowing, and everywhere all at once *(and He certainly doesn't play favorites)*! Everyone experiences seasons of success or chaos—but regardless of our circumstances, we must navigate the hand we're dealt with joy and excellence.

One of my girlfriends from high school, Leah, worked hard to become a highly esteemed lawyer and a self-made millionaire. However, her accomplishments had nothing to do with "luck" or receiving a "good hand." She intentionally rose above every letdown, roadblock, naysayer, and curveball—and she is now passionate about encouraging others to do the same. Her confidence advice is simple:

1. No more couch potato! Embracing a more active lifestyle produces energy and clarity, and it stimulates endorphins that lead to happier, wiser decisions!
2. Speak kindly and positively! If you wouldn't say it to someone else, don't say it to yourself!
3. Surround yourself with people who believe in you more than you believe in yourself!
4. Comparison is useless. Let it go!
5. Step out of circles that stunt your growth or cause you to play small by tiptoeing around the insecurities of others!

The plans God has for you are good—however, we are not His robots! It's up to us to live with gratitude, walk by faith, and shine bright in this topsy-turvy life!

> God, I know luck has nothing to do with living a fulfilled life. I choose to learn through every misfortune and always display an attitude of praise. Amen.

# Victory over Victimhood

*Now a certain man was there
who had an infirmity thirty-eight years.
When Jesus saw him lying there, and knew
that he had already been in that condition a long time,
He said to him, "Do you want to be made well?"
The sick man answered Him, "Sir, I have no man
to put me into the pool when the water is stirred up."*
JOHN 5:5-7 NKJV

For most children, there's something oddly attractive about having a minor injury. Whether it's wearing a big Cinderella Band-Aid, sporting a lopsided arm sling, or carrying a massive set of crutches, these new accessories give us a twinge of excitement. Why? Because all eyes will be on us! Even though the injury itself wasn't fun, this temporary state of woundedness invites attention from others—making us feel seen, known, and loved in an unusual way. I even remember getting excited after a bad sunburn because I could display my redness like a badge of honor and show off my impressive peeling skills *(gross, I know)*.

Victimhood, in a strange way, can be enticing. When we break a bone, our friends line up to sign the cast. When we experience tough times, we are inundated with food, flowers, and finances. When we post our problems on social media, we are flooded with positive comments and engagement. No, we don't enjoy the suffering—but we do enjoy being on the receiving end of kindness. However, there is a caveat to this: *We must never set up camp in the valley simply because we're addicted to the attention we receive while we're there.*

Today's Bible passage is a good example of this. I'm sure the man didn't enjoy being sick for thirty-eight years, but his response to Jesus was telling: it showed he preferred pity rather than healing. Instead of coddling the man's victimhood, Jesus boldly told him to get up, pick up his mat, and walk—and at once, the man was healed.

Life is hard, and it's okay to receive kindness and grace. But if we prefer encouragement and affirmation more than we prefer healing and restoration, it will never produce God's best for our lives. Walking in victory suffocates a victim mentality, and that leads to a confidence that changes everything!

> God, I want healing more than anything! I choose to get up, pick up my mat, and walk. Amen.

# Restore the Sparkle

*Turn and answer me, O Lord my God!*
*Restore the sparkle to my eyes.*

**PSALM 13:3 NLT**

For Christmas, my sister gave me an ultrasonic jewelry cleaner. I placed my jewelry inside the container, added cleaning fluid, plugged it in, and watched the magic happen. My rings started shaking so violently that the song "Hips Don't Lie" by Shakira started randomly playing in my head—but then I started laughing, because it reminded me of a time in high school when I secretly changed my mom's ringtone to that song. One day, it rang so loudly in line at the grocery store that *everyone* stared. She was *so* confused, and I was *so* amused.

Anyway—back to the jewelry cleaner. Once the cycle was complete, I couldn't believe the amount of filth floating around inside the container. It looked like a combination of belly-button lint and fingernail dirt, if I'm being honest. After removing my rings and rinsing off the soap and leftover grime, their sparkle was radiantly restored to its original brilliance.

It's easy for us to sparkle and shine when there are no relationship issues, no stresses at work, no negative balances in the bank, and no problems within our bodies. However, that's a dream world we simply don't live in! The germs, dirt, and grime of life can dull our spirits, making it extremely hard to shine with confidence.

The wonderful thing about choosing Jesus is we are no longer responsible for carrying our filth. Choosing Jesus makes us new—it restores our souls to their original purity and brilliance. However, there are times when we need an ultrasonic kind of cleaning—when God shakes us up a little bit in order to remove things within our character that don't belong!

Getting our sparkle back means going to the Lord with an honest, humble heart. It means looking at God and not our circumstances, recognizing His goodness and remembering His faithfulness through every trial, battle, and valley. He is exactly the ultrasonic cleaner we need—one that refines our hearts and washes us white as snow.

May you allow Him to restore your sparkle. He brings a confidence that changes everything and allows you to shine bright in this topsy-turvy life!

*God, thank You for
the cleansing blood of Jesus.
Remove the grime in my life and let
Your Spirit shine through me. Amen.*

# Guilt-Free Confidence

*Finally, I confessed all my sins to You and stopped trying to hide my guilt. I said to myself, "I will confess my rebellion to the L<small>ORD</small>." And You forgave me! All my guilt is gone.*

PSALM 32:5 NLT

We had a pretty intense near-drowning incident with my son once. I was a total dodo-head and took off his floaty prematurely while packing up to leave a pool party. I walked inside for just a moment, only for us to realize that every adult was inside too. I bolted out the door and frightfully found my son submerged underwater. Thankfully, our little rascal was fine. He was conscious and hadn't inhaled water. But gosh, guys—the level of guilt I carried after that incident was debilitating. Beating myself up was a daily thing; it stole my sleep and haunted my thoughts so much that I could barely look at myself in the mirror. While I was grateful the Lord spared my son's life, I didn't believe I deserved that kind of mercy. Any "mommy confidence" I once had went sayonara. Bye-bye. Peace out, homies.

We all struggle with debilitating guilt over something we've done. Whether it was a total accident, a bad habit, an ill intention, or a personality flaw, there are things from our past that make us cringe and shudder with regret. How are we supposed to walk in confidence if we loathe the mere reflection of our actions or character?

First of all, guilt is not our portion, and it certainly does not come from the Lord. When we humble ourselves to the Lord and express remorse for our mistakes, regardless if those mistakes were intentional or not, He clothes us with mercy and forgiveness and forgets it altogether.

Second of all, the guilt of your past does not hinder God's will for your life, nor does it mean you've missed it. Scripture is clear: God's will for you is to rejoice always, pray continually, and give thanks in all circumstances (I Thessalonians 5:16-18). His will for you is to act justly, to love mercy, and to walk humbly (Micah 6:8). No matter what you've been carrying, it hasn't affected God's will for your life one stinkin' bit!

God is not out to get you. *He is for you.* You've been absolved from guilt, and that brings a confidence that changes everything!

> God, thank You for
> loving me even when I didn't
> love myself. Amen.

# The Only Way

*There is salvation in no one else!*
*God has given no other name under heaven*
*by which we must be saved.*

**ACTS 4:12 NLT**

I grew up in a Christian home. We went to church every Sunday. My siblings and I attended Christian school and went on more mission trips than I can count. However, was that enough to convince me that Jesus was the only way to heaven? Not really.

In fact, when life got hard, that's when I began to question things. I finally started looking for answers instead of taking everybody's word for it. I read the Bible for myself and sought God for myself, filtered through my own theology of what was true and what was not. And, like most people, I wondered, *How can I be confident that Jesus is the* only way *to heaven with so many religions out there? If God is so good, why are humans allowed only one pathway to receive eternal life?*

These are all valid questions, ones that the Lord welcomes. But what if we changed our perspective and started asking questions like this:

- Why would God, with as horribly messed up and sinful as we are, allow *any pathway at all* for us to experience heaven?

- Why would God, with as flawless and holy as He is, want *us* to live with *Him* forever if we're constantly breaking His heart?

It's a love I definitely don't understand. Because if someone breaks my heart, I certainly don't forget. But yet, God sent Jesus—His perfect Son—to take the death penalty for my shortcomings. This incredible act of love means that through Jesus, I can be forgiven and made pure, "washed white as snow." That's unreal!

It's not a matter of "Why would a good God *not accept* everyone into heaven?" It's a matter of why He would choose to give sinners like us a chance in the first place. God presents us with countless, numerous, plentiful opportunities to surrender our lives to Christ throughout our lifetime. That's *grace*, and to me, that proves that *He is good!*

God has never stopped pursuing me, and He certainly will never stop pursuing you. Yes, there is only one way to heaven—but the fact that He gave us a way at all brings us a confidence that changes everything!

> God, I can't believe You love me like that. Thank You for sending Your Son. I surrender my life to You, now and forever. Amen.

# A Confidence That Changes Everything

*For I am sure that neither death nor life, nor angels nor rulers, nor things present nor things to come, nor powers, nor height nor depth, nor anything else in all creation, will be able to separate us from the love of God in Christ Jesus our Lord.*

ROMANS 8:38-39 ESV

This is our ninetieth devotion together. Wowzas! For you to have read every single one of these pages shows me one thing: *you are hungry for the things of God*. You might also be hungry for some Chick-fil-A right now, and if that's the case, finish this book and go grab you some nuggs. You deserve the Lord's chicken.

This journey has walked us down some trails that, I'm sure, you weren't expecting. But if you take away anything from this book, let it be these three things:

1. Confidence is found when you surrender your character, your mind, and your life to Christ.
2. Confidence is found when you daily seek His face.
3. Confidence is found when you see yourself, and others, the way He does.

Confidence isn't about discovering what makes you

*you*, it's about discovering *the God who made you*. And there is truly no way to find genuine, authentic confidence outside of Jesus.

You know me, I can't finish a devotional like this without giving you one last opportunity to receive Jesus as your personal Lord and Savior. Even if you've already prayed a prayer like this before, I encourage you to pray it with me again. Let's use this time together to honor the Lord for not only Who He is but for what He is continuing to do within *you*!

> God, my soul longs for You. I simply cannot ignore it any longer. There is no way I can walk confidently in life without You leading and guiding my every step. Today, I choose to devote my entire self to You—to loving You, to learning about You, and to becoming more like You. I believe, God, that You sent Your Son Jesus to die for my sins, and I believe He is alive today. Holy Spirit, fill my heart. Change me, mold me, and make me a vessel for Your glory. Amen.

The Alpha and the Omega. The Beginning and the End. He alone is the One who gives a confidence that changes everything.

LIVE YOUR FAITH

*Dear Friend,*

This book was prayerfully crafted with you, the reader, in mind. Every word, every sentence, every page was thoughtfully written, designed, and packaged to encourage you—right where you are this very moment. At DaySpring, our vision is to see every person experience the life-changing message of God's love. So, as we worked through rough drafts, design changes, edits, and details, we prayed for you to deeply experience His unfailing love, indescribable peace, and pure joy. It is our sincere hope that through these Truth-filled pages your heart will be blessed, knowing that God cares about you—your desires and disappointments, your challenges and dreams.

*He knows. He cares. He loves you unconditionally.*

**BLESSINGS!**
**THE DAYSPRING BOOK TEAM**

---

Additional copies of this book and
other DaySpring titles can be purchased
at fine retailers everywhere.
Order online at <u>dayspring.com</u>
or
by phone at 1-877-751-4347